D1486782

DOMESTIC ABUSERS
Terrorists in Our Homes

ABOUT THE AUTHOR

Sara Lee Johann, an attorney, resides in Cedarburg, Wisconsin. She is the author of two prior books, *Representing... Battered Women Who Kill,* and *Sourcebook on Pornography* (the national encyclopedia against pornography). Johann, the former director of a battered woman center, trains professionals, presents lectures, and consults in cases involving domestic violence, battered women who kill their abuser, pornography/obscenity/imitative violence, and child abuse.

DOMESTIC ABUSERS
TERRORISTS IN OUR HOMES

By

SARA LEE JOHANN, J.D.

CHARLES C THOMAS • PUBLISHER
Springfield • Illinois • U.S.A.

Published and Distributed Throughout the World by

CHARLES C THOMAS • PUBLISHER
2600 South First Street
Springfield, Illinois 62794-9265

© *1994 by* CHARLES C THOMAS • PUBLISHER

ISBN 0-398-05904-7

Library of Congress Catalog Card Number: 93-47036

Printed in the United States of America
SC-R-3

Library of Congress Cataloging-in-Publication Data

Johann, Sara Lee.
    Domestic abusers : terrorists in our homes / Sara Lee Johann.
        p.   cm.
    Includes bibliographical references and index.
    ISBN 0-398-05904-7 (alk. paper)
    1. Family violence. 2. Abused women.   3. Family violence—
Psychological aspects.   4. Family violence—Prevention.   5. Abused
women—Psychology.   I. Title.
HQ809.J64   1994
362.82'92—dc20
                                                          93-47036
                                                             CIP

DEDICATION

To Michael, for inspiring me to write this book, and helping me to find the strength to do so.

And to the many women and men who have been battered, abused, or sexually assaulted by their mates who, like me, have found or must find the courage to either end the abusive relationship or end the abuse in the relationship, and who have found or will find the strength to go forward with their lives—SURROUNDED BY LOVE.

Justice, like lasting love, is rare but not impossible. Both depend on the courage and diligence of one enlightened person.

Jean le Malchanceux
A Crusader's Journal

CONTENTS

r

DOMESTIC ABUSERS
Terrorists in Our Homes

Chapter 1

THE "LOOK" OF A WOMAN
ABUSED BY HER MATE

I am looking at you now.

I wonder what you see.

I am willing to bet that the "me" you think you know, the "me" you think you see is not the real me.

Do you see through my carefully orchestrated false image which I present in public to glance into my real, inner self? I do this to preserve what little remains of my own self-esteem. And to hide the truth from the outside world. In all honesty, I bury the truth some place deep within my own conscience, in a place where it will be forgotten, forgiven, ignored, so that I can pretend that he never battered me, physically or emotionally. I simply block it out of my mind. I tell myself it never happened. Or that it's all my own fault. Not his.

He has promised to change his abusive behavior. And I believe him.

Is the fear I live with every moment of every day well-enough hidden? Or do you notice it lurking in the depths of my soulful eyes?

I hope that you do not sense, or see that there is anything wrong.

I have managed to cover up my bruises. Again. Utilizing an expertise at makeup and disguise which I would never have believed myself capable of. The long sleeved shirt, and long pants, worn on a hot summer day cover the bruises on my arms and legs. Bruises put there when my mate struck me with his fists and kicked me with the hard toes of his boots. This is not the first time something like this has happened to me. I keep hoping it will be the last.

The bruises, the pain caused by his sexual abuse of me are invisible to the world. Invisible to you. Unless I were to tell you about this. That I will not do. It is one of the most humiliating, embarrassing, and terrorizing aspects of my relationship with him.

3

I have developed dark circles under my pain-filled eyes from the restlessness and lack of sleep caused by living in fear of this man. I have used a cover-up stick (an appropriate name) to disguise the circles.

On those occasions when he has given me a black eye I also wear dark glasses. If he has struck my face it takes a heavy coat of makeup to hide the bruises. I have become skilled at doing this. For it seems as if I have no choice.

I suppose I tolerate his abuse because I love him. I fear losing him more than I fear his abuse.

It does worry me that lately I have been daydreaming about killing him to end the violence. But I don't believe in that sort of thing. Truly I don't.

Do you sense the cause of the stress which manifests itself in my shaking hands?

Have I taken enough aspirin today to reduce the physical pain? Enough antidepressants prescribed by my doctor to keep me from ending my own life?

I've thought about that, too.

But I have to think about the children. The children need me. Their mother. They depend on me. And I love them very deeply.

I fear that he may kill or injure the children one day.

I would never let him do that.

I look at you—a friend, a relative, a stranger, a neighbor, a coworker, a trained professional, and I wonder how obvious my inner distress is.

It scares me that you can look at me and not even begin to sense the terror, the hopelessness, the fear, the powerlessness, the physical and emotional pain that I experience every moment of every day.

How can this reality be so invisible to you.

While it totally consumes me.

Until there is nothing left of my soul except a pitiful and empty shell. Of what I used to be.

Yet I am unable to call out to you for help.

Part of me keeps hoping that you will recognize me as a battered woman and a victim of sexual abuse and of emotional terrorism caused by my own mate.

He's got a terrific image in the community. Everybody thinks we're the perfect couple.

You see nothing.

My phony image of happiness, stability, calm, has been so successful that you do not even begin to sense the truth. It is the only thing I
have succeeded at in a long, long time.

You would probably never believe how down I am toward myself.

Because I appear so "up" whenever I see you.

How can you be so blind?

By the time you see me the way I really am, it may be too late.

I may be dead.

I fear that he will eventually kill me. In one of his outbursts of
murderous rage.

There is nothing I can do to protect myself from him. He is so much
bigger and stronger than I.

If you look closely enough, you will notice that I am different from
other women.

You will see the fear, the sadness, the hurt, and the hopelessness in
my eyes. You will notice my lack of self-esteem and my inability to
function normally. Won't you?

If you saw me the way I really am, would you help me to end the
abuse?

If I reached out to you for help, would you respond?

Deep down, I think I recognize that his violence toward me will
never stop until I expose his abusive behavior to the light of day.

You will help me, won't you?

I desperately need somebody to believe me.

Somebody to care.

As I look into your eyes and realize that you do suspect that I am an
abused woman, that you do see the deep-felt pain I am suffering, I
know I have to tell you the truth about his violence toward me.

I know that you will help me to end the abuse.

Because I know that you truly do care.

Chapter 2

BATTERED WOMEN AND BATTERERS: LIVES HOPELESSLY OUT OF CONTROL

B attered women and those professionals who provide them with help in the form of counseling, legal advice, restraining orders, safety, arrest and prosecution of abusers, financial aid, and other services need to be aware of the fact that many women who have been the victims of sustained physical and psychological abuse by their mate suffer from the Battered Woman syndrome.

The Battered Woman syndrome is a sociological theory of the effects a sustained pattern of physical, psychological, and often sexual, abuse over time from the male in the husband/boyfriend role in a woman's life has upon the abused woman. The syndrome consists of the common characteristics that battered women share and the common characteristics that batterers share.

Professionals who become involved in cases where battered women have killed their abuser should be aware that such women no longer suffer from the effects of such abuse once the batterer is dead and is no longer a threat to their physical safety or psychological health. Therefore, in helping these women to make out effective arguments that they killed their abusers in self-defense, or while suffering from a mental disease or defect, the behavior and attitudes of the women prior to the time of the abuser's death must be thoroughly examined.

Professionals who become involved with women who are still engaged in relationships with their abusers should be aware that the behavior patterns and attitudes of these women are the result of their suffering from the Battered Woman syndrome, and that such cases must be approached from the viewpoint of dealing with someone who is experiencing the symptoms of that sociological syndrome.

Characteristics of Battered Women

The following information is taken primarily from a brief this author wrote on behalf of Barbara Lange, a battered woman who killed her abusive husband, Peter Lange, in self-defense in DuPage County, Illinois, in 1989.

The characteristics of battered women include: fear, economic dependence on the batterer, emotional dependence on the batterer, guilt (blaming themselves for the batterer's actions), the belief that no one can help them unless they themselves improve, that the batterer is omnipotent (a distorted perception that is part of the reason they believe no one can help them), and isolation.

(See: Sara Lee Johann, et. al., *Representing... Battered Women Who Kill* (Springfield, Illinois: Charles C Thomas, Publisher, 1989), pp. 27–46; Charles Patrick Ewing, *Battered Women Who Kill: Psychological Self-Defense As Legal Justification* (Lexington, Massachusetts: Lexington Books, 1987), pp. 7–21; Angela Browne, *When Battered Women Kill* (New York: The Free Press, 1987); Lenore Walker, *The Battered Women* (New York: Harper and Row, 1979); Lenore Walker, *The Battered Woman Syndrome* (New York: Springer, 1984); Jeffrey Robinson, "Defense Strategies for Battered Women Who Assault Their Mates: State v. Curry," 4 *Harvard Women's Law Journal*, 1981, 161–175, at 163; Nancy Fiora-Gormally, "Battered Wives Who Kill: Double Standard Out of Court, Single Standard In?", 1978 *Law and Human Behavior*, 1978, 133–165, 152–153; Roberta K. Thyfault, "Self-Defense: Battered Woman Syndrome on Trial," 20 *California Western Law Review*, Spring, 1984, 485–510, at 486–491; Elizabeth M. Schneider, "Describing and Changing: Women's Self-Defense Work and the Problem of Expert Testimony on Battering," 9 *Women's Rights Law Reporter*, 195–222, at 63–66; Colleen Cacy, "The Battered Woman's Syndrome Defense," 34 *Kansas Law Review* 1985, 339–366, at 339–346; Jimmie E. Tinsley, "Criminal Law: The Battered Woman Defense," 34 *American Jurisprudence Proof of Facts, Second Series,* 1–60, at 10–12; M. Julianne Leary, "A Woman, A Horse, and a Hickory Tree: The Development of Expert Testimony on the Battered Woman Syndrome in Homicide Cases," 53 (3) *University of Missouri Kansas City Law Review* 1985, 386–410, at 397–400.)

There are many reasons why battered women do not leave their abusers. They include:

1. The woman may have no safe place to go. The shelter may be full,

unavailable, or available only for a few weeks. She may or may not feel safe remaining in her own home (and having the batterer kept away by getting a domestic abuse restraining order and its enforcement if he violates it).

2. Economic. Even if the abused woman works, she might not have enough income, absent the batterer's income, to support herself and her children. She may not qualify for welfare. She might need to get divorced and obtain court orders for child support and/or alimony before she is financially able to survive. She may not have the money to institute the divorce process. If she needs to hide from the batterer, a divorce would require her to see him in court and could result in his being granted the right to visit his children.

3. Fear. The abused woman may fear for her own life, for those of her children, and for the lives of other family members or friends. Her abuser may have threatened to kill them, or, just as commonly, to kill himself, if she leaves. He may have attempted to kill her during a prior incident of abuse.

4. Battered women are usually so busy surviving day to day that they do not make long-term plans.

5. The battered woman may have been severely beaten because she left the abuser before. Therefore, she may be terrified that the same thing will happen if she leaves again.

6. It may be easier to remain in a familiar situation than to continue to live with the same fear of abuse by the batterer—if he shows up at her home or job after she left him.

7. The violence may not end when the relationship ends.

8. The abused woman may hope the batterer will change. She may believe that things truly will get better if she tries harder to improve the relationship.

9. She loves the abuser. (This, in the view of the author, is a major reason why battered women remain with their abusers. See Chapter 4 for a detailed exploration of this aspect of abusive relationships.)

10. The battered woman believes she cannot survive on her own. This is a result of the batterer's having brainwashed her into believing that he is in complete control of their lives, that he makes all decisions, that he is omnipotent. He has helped to enforce that inaccurate belief in her mind by isolating her from friends, family, and, in some cases, cutting off her ability to earn an income on her own.

11. Sometimes leaving doesn't help. The abuser may keep coming

back. A batterer may kill a battered woman while they are living together or after they have ended the relationship. It is up to our criminal justice system to see to it that batterers leave their victims alone. The chances of a batterer killing a battered woman because she has left him are still relatively rare compared to the overall number of cases where women have been abused. The chance of being killed by a batterer if an abused woman remains in an abusive relationship are also rare. Abuse should not be tolerated, in any case.

(See Johann's *Representing . . . Battered Women Who Kill,* pp. 27–46.)

Loraine Patricia Eber named the following reasons why battered women remain in battering relationships in "The Battered Wife's Dilemma: To Kill or To Be Killed," 32 *Hastings Law Journal,* March, 1981, 895–931, at 901–902:

1. Emotional dependency on her assailant and on the marriage (i.e., or intimate relationship) itself.

2. Sex-role conditioning which causes women to bear the burden for the success of the marriage—makes her feel guilty about the beatings and give the batterer innumerable second chances.

3. Low self-esteem.

4. Fear of the husband.

5. Some women feel they deserve the beatings.

6. Shame.

7. Lack of confidence to reach out to people who would be able to help with problems.

8. Fear of reprisals from an angry spouse.

9. Economic dependency (lack of marketable skills, unemployment, child care problems, lack of access to family bank accounts, lack of money).

10. A false hope that the abuser will reform.

11. The fear for the safety or well-being of their children.

12. Having no place to go. Being unaware of the shelters which are available for battered women.

Eber's sources for her reasons why battered women do not leave batterers included such well-known and widely-cited books as Del Martin's *Battered Wives* (San Francisco, California: Glide, 1976), pp. 81–82, 84, 76, and 78, and M. Roy's *Battered Women,* 1977, pp. 115, 81–82, and 31.

Fiora-Gormally, at 152–153 describes other characteristics of battered women:

First, such women are females. Female roles in our culture require women to be "submissive, dependent, passive, receptive, gentle, quiet, nonaggressive, home-oriented, not at all ambitious or competitive, and possessed of scant or no combative strength."

Second, she is often a wife, and often has children. She is economically and socially dependent on her husband. She believes she "cannot make it alone without him." If employed, her job is secondary to her primary role as a mother and a wife. She usually retains responsibility for home chores and management even if she works. Her intimate sexual experiences "may be tied exclusively to her husband." She "is subordinate to him." The battered woman may also believe, like a substantial portion of the population does, that he has a right to strike her.

Third, she is a battered wife. She is often beaten. The beatings are unpredictable. They increase in severity. She is powerless to stop the abuse. She is trapped in the relationship. Sociopsychological pressures oppose her leaving him. The legal system does not work for her. She "has nowhere to go and no money to facilitate departure." The battered woman "lives in a state of mounting, intensifying fear, a state of cumulative terror," Fiora-Gormally concludes.

In *State v. Hodges,* 716 P.2d 563, 566, 239 Kan. 63 (Kan., 1986), Dr. Ann Bristow, an expert witness, called the Battered Woman syndrome "a post-traumatic stress disorder with the particular stressor being wife abuse." She described the symptoms of the disorder:

> Symptoms manifested by a woman suffering from the syndrome include an attempt to minimize the violence and to live for the positive aspects of the relationship. She lives in a highly fearful state, becoming very sensitive to when the situation is becoming more violent and to those things that precede arguments. The batterer isolates the woman and will not allow her to go places, and she becomes more and more withdrawn. Few women will discuss their problems even with close family members because of their feeling that nothing can be done about the situation. They have a "learned helplessness"; the more the repeated trauma occurs, the more the woman learns she has no control.

As society studies battered women and learns more and more about their common patterns of suffering and behavior and attitudes, we will be able to better help these women to end the abuse in their lives. What we already know should help us to identify and help battered women, and should help battered women to recognize themselves as battered women. In a nation where experts anticipate that millions of women will, unfortunately, experience physical and/or sexual abuse by their mates, those who have been subjected to such harm should not feel alone in their plight. They must reach out to others who have had such experiences and have survived, and to professionals who can help them to overcome the abusive situation and to move forward with their lives.

The Cycle Theory of Violence

While there is some dispute among experts who work with victims and perpetrators of domestic violence regarding whether abuse takes place in battering cycles, the "Cycle Theory of Violence" is still a widely accepted belief about battering relationships.

Lenore Walker developed this theory in her book, *The Battered Woman,* pp. 55–70. She stated that violent behavior takes place in three separate repetitive stages which vary in intensity and duration for different individuals, the *Kelly* court noted. It, at 371–372, described Walker's theory of violence:

> Phase one of the battering cycle is referred to as the "tension-building stage," during which the battering male engages in minor battering incidents and verbal abuse while the woman, beset by fear and tension, attempts to be as placating and passive as possible in order to stave off more serious violence. *Id. at 56–59.*

> Phase two of the battering cycle is the "acute battering incident." At some point during phase one, the tension between the battered woman and the batterer becomes intolerable and more serious violence inevitable. The triggering event that initiates phase two is most often an internal or external event in the life of the battering male, but provocation for more severe violence is sometimes provided by the woman who can no longer tolerate or control her phase-one anger and anxiety. *Id. at 59–65.*

> Phase three of the battering cycle is characterized by extreme contrition and loving behavior on the part of the battering male. During this period the man will often mix his pleas for forgiveness and protestations of devotion with promises to seek professional help, to stop drinking, and to refrain from further violence. For some couples, this period of relative calm may last as long as several months, but in a battering relationship the affection and contrition of the man will eventually fade and phase one of the cycle will start anew. *Id. at 65–70.*

> The cyclical nature of battering behavior helps explain why more women simply do not leave their abusers. The loving behavior demonstrated by the batterer during phase three reinforces whatever hopes these women might have for their mate's reform and keeps them bound to the relationship. *R. Langley and R. Levy, Wife Beating: The Silent Crisis 112–14 (1977).*

> Some women may even perceive the battering cycle as normal, especially if

they grew up in a violent household. *Battered Women, a Psychosociological Study of Domestic Violence 670 (M. Roy, ed. 1977); D. Martin, Battered Wives, 60 (1981).*

One attack on the cycle theory of violence has been the argument that the cycle often ends by the women ending the relationship eventually, or getting killed by the batterer, or killing the batterer. However, in the viewpoint of this author, the cycle theory remains a relatively accurate description of the typical pattern which takes place in domestically abusive relationships.

Lack of Options for Battered Women: One Major Reason Why They Remain in Abusive Relationships

A major reason why many battered women remain with abusive men is that they lack reasonable options and alternatives. Many of these victims are financially unable to support themselves and their children alone. Financial self-sufficiency is needed to enable battered women to get their abusive mates out of their lives.

This is a societal problem. It goes far beyond the issue in individual cases of domestic abuse of separating the parties or taking appropriate steps to keep them together by changing the nature of the relationship into a nonabusive one. We, as a society, in our duty to ensure the safety, health, and welfare of its members, and in our duty to seek and ensure justice, owe it to these battered women to find ways to help them gain financial independence. Society needs to focus on the following types of issues in order to help battered women end the violence in their lives:

1. Job availability, referrals, and training.

2. Making affordable child care much more available to mothers while paying decent wages to child care providers.

3. Enforcement of child support laws and orders (including crackdowns on unreported income sources).

4. Better wages and working conditions for employees.

5. Wage equity for women.

6. Better pay for jobs that women are traditionally forced into such as secretarial/office work, waitressing, low-wage factory jobs, nursing, and sales clerking.

7. Opening up job opportunities for women in the better paying jobs and jobs which carry decision-making authority (such as corporate executives, politically powerful positions, etc.)

8. Improving the overall U.S. economy so that more and better jobs become available.

9. Self-reliance skills and attitudes.

10. Fighting poverty and its causes.

11. Reducing discrimination against women and minorities.

12. Education.

13. Housing options, including more affordable housing.

14. Longer-term shelters, or housing for victims of domestic violence.

15. Sharing resources. For example, one woman might be skilled at house cleaning, another at child care, a third at writing, a fourth at fixing appliances, etc.

16. Willingness to accept less well-off lifestyles (at least temporarily) in exchange for the safety and tranquility of ending the abuse.

Until we, as a society, face up to the fact that we need to seek and provide reasonable living options for battered women who want to end their abusive relationships, we face a future in which more and more women continue to be trapped, through no fault of their own, in intimate relationships which can only be described as the equivalent of experiencing terrorism in their own homes.

We owe it to these women to try as hard as we can to help them out of these life-threatening situations.

Do Battered Women Suffer From Psychological Problems?

Another debate which rages within the movement against domestic violence is the issue of whether battered women suffer from psychological problems. Radical feminists tend to argue that such women do not have psychological disorders. Those experts, such as the author, who have had to deal with the courtroom strategy of defending battered women who kill their abusers, argue and believe that at least some battered women do, indeed, suffer from the sociological syndrome known as the Battered Woman syndrome (described above, and in Chapter 5), and, in some cases, the psychological disorders set forth in the *Diagnostic and Statistical Manual of Mental Disorders* (Third Edition-Revised), Washington, D.C.: American Psychiatric Association, 1987, known as the Borderline Personality Disorder and the Post Traumatic Stress Disorder. The following diagnostic criteria for those disorders are reprinted from the *Desk Reference to the Diagnostic and Statistical Manual of Mental Disorders.*

The fact that a particular woman suffered from a mental disease or defect at the time she killed her abuser (even if in self-defense) is an important defense which must be explored and, in some cases, pursued and presented, by the attorneys and expert witnesses who are helping her to defeat typically inappropriate charges of murder or manslaughter brought against her by prosecutors.

Beyond that, this author would argue that we need to recognize and deal realistically with the fact that battered women often do indeed suffer from psychological problems which are caused by their batterers' systematic and lengthy abuse of them. This is not something for these women to be ashamed of. It is something which must be realistically dealt with and cured. For us, as professionals, and as a caring society, to close our eyes to the reality that battered women experience psychological problems is like sticking our heads in the sand. It would be far wiser to recognize this aspect of battering relationships and to address it instead of ignoring it. Ignored problems do not go away.

301.83 Borderline Personality Disorder
A pervasive pattern of instability of mood, interpersonal relationships, and self-image, beginning by early adulthood and present in a variety of contexts, as indicated by at least *five* of the following:

(1) a pattern of unstable and intense interpersonal relationships characterized by alternating between extremes of overidealization and devaluation

(2) impulsiveness in at least two areas that are potentially self-damaging, e.g., spending, sex, substance use, shoplifting, reckless driving, binge eating (Do not include suicidal or self-mutilating behavior covered in (5).)

(3) affective instability: marked shifts from baseline mood to depression, irritability, or anxiety, usually lasting a few hours and only rarely more than a few days

(4) inappropriate, intense anger or lack of control of anger, e.g., frequent displays of temper, constant anger, recurrent physical behavior

(5) recurrent suicidal threats, gestures, or behavior, or self-mutilating behavior

(6) marked and persistent identity disturbance manifested by uncertainty about at least two of the following: self-image, sexual orientation, long-term goals or career choice, type of friends desired, preferred values

(7) chronic feelings of emptiness or boredom

(8) frantic efforts to avoid real or imagined abandonment (Do not include suicidal or self-mutilating behavior covered in (5).) (pp. 194–195)

309.89 Post-Traumatic Stress Disorder

A. The person has experienced an event that is outside the range of usual human experience that would be markedly distressing to almost anyone, e.g., serious threat to one's life or physical integrity; serious threat or harm to one's children, spouse, or other close relatives and friends;

sudden destruction of one's home or community; or seeing another person who has recently been, or is being, seriously injured or killed as the result of an accident or physical violence.

B. The traumatic event is persistently re-experienced in at least one of the following ways:

    (1) recurrent and intrusive distressing recollections of the event (in young children, repetitive play in which themes or aspects of the trauma are expressed)

    (2) recurrent distressing dreams of the event

    (3) sudden acting or feeling as if the traumatic event were recurring (includes a sense of reliving the experience, illusions, hallucinations, and dissociative (flashback) episodes, even those that occur upon awakening or when intoxicated)

    (4) intense psychological distress at exposure to events that symbolize or resemble an aspect of the traumatic event, including anniversaries of the trauma

C. Persistent avoidance of stimuli associated with the trauma or numbing of general responsiveness (not present before the trauma), as indicated by at least three of the following:

    (1) efforts to avoid thoughts or feelings associated with the trauma

    (2) efforts to avoid activities or situations that arouse recollections of the trauma

    (3) inability to recall an important aspect of the trauma (psychogenic amnesia)

    (4) markedly diminished interest in significant activities (in young children, loss of recently acquired developmental skills such as toilet training or language skills)

    (5) feeling of detachment or estrangement from others

    (6) restricted range of affect, e.g., unable to have loving feelings

    (7) sense of foreshortened future, e.g., does not expect to have a career, marriage, or children, or a long life

D. Persistent symptoms of increased arousal (not present before the trauma), as indicated by at least two of the following:

    (1) difficulty falling or staying asleep

    (2) irritability or outbursts of anger

    (3) difficulty concentrating

    (4) hypervigilance

    (5) exaggerated startle response

    (6) physiologic reactivity upon exposure to events that symbolize or resemble an aspect of the traumatic event (e.g., a woman who was raped in an elevator breaks out in a sweat when entering any elevator)

E. Duration of the disturbance (symptoms in B, C, and D) of at least one month.

    Specify delayed onset if the onset of symptoms was at least six months after the trauma." (pp. 146–148)

In conclusion, we are only fooling ourselves if we fail to deal with the emotions experienced by battered women in addition to treating their physical injuries. While the physical injuries may, at least in some cases, present much danger to these women, the emotional and psychological injuries done to them on a day-to-day basis by their abusers present at least as great a threat to their long-term psychological, emotional, and physical well-being.

(Author's Note: The Battered Woman syndrome discussed earlier in this chapter is not complete without adding to the characteristics of abused women, the characteristics of batterers. The characteristics of batterers discussed in Chapter 5 should be added to the characteristics of abused women from this chapter when determining whether a particular woman suffers from the Battered Woman syndrome.)

Chapter 3

LIVING WITH AN ABUSIVE MATE IS LIKE
LIVING THROUGH HELL ON EARTH

The following segments of the book are written from the standpoint of victims of domestic abuse with a purpose of helping others to understand what these women experience in abusive relationships.

The Emotional Abuse Is Devastating

As I reflect back upon the years in which I remained with my domestic abuser, I have come to the realization that his emotional abuse of me played a major role in keeping me in the relationship.

This is true because the emotional abuse destroyed my self-esteem and my ability to function aside and apart from the batterer.

In fact, I have heard from some other victims of domestic abuse that sometimes domestic abuse cases consist entirely of emotional abuse. However, I cautioned these women that their verbal abuse could escalate into physical abuse such as battery or sexual assault. Because my abuse started out as emotional abuse, too.

My abuser frequently yelled at me. This kept me in a constant state of nervousness, jumpiness, and stress. It made me uncertain how to act, and unable to make decisions for fear of upsetting him. There were also times when his verbal abuse preceded his physical or sexual abuse of me. His yelling kept me in a constant state of fear regarding the potential for physical abuse as well.

He was insecure and lacked self-worth. Instead of taking steps to improve his own mental attitude, he constantly subjected me to put-downs:

He attacked my weight, physical appearance, manner of dress. I was always too fat, no matter how much weight I lost. I was never as pretty as the glamour girls in his pornographic magazines. And the form-fitting dresses these models wore never looked good on me because I just didn't have the physical shape (bust, waist, hips) that he wanted in his ideal

17

woman. Of course, few women would fit his concept of how a mate should look. I did not realize that at the time. It seemed as if there was something wrong with me. Not with him.

He called me stupid. And that hurt. I wasn't stupid. I had a college degree. And the abilities that went with it. I gave up a lot of professional job opportunities to maintain a household and raise children. For him. For us, I suppose.

Yet he attacked my skills like child care, cooking, cleaning, and other household duties he should have been doing his share of. Nothing I did was ever good enough for him. So, I will admit, there were times when I was too terrified to do anything. But that seemed to make him angry, too.

He used to compare me, always in negative ways, to other women he knew: his old girlfriends, his sisters, his school classmates, the women he worked with at his fancy job, even to movie actresses. This made me feel insecure and worthless.

Which describes my general feeling toward life at the time anyway.

It hurt when he would attack my sexual attractiveness and say I was not able to arouse him. This just wasn't true. I could tell when a man was aroused. There was no doubt that *he* was. But I admit I hated some of the demeaning sexual acts he would force me to perform. He would accuse me of not being attracted to him. I suppose in a way that this became true—after his verbal and physical and sexual abuse made me stop wanting to be intimate with him.

He suggested I do things, such as work, which are far beneath my training and education.

He called me worthless.

And treated me like someone he considered worthless. An object. Not a human being with real feelings and human needs.

I remember how emotionally devastating it was when he would cut me down in public, or in front of friends, family, and business associates. Looking back, I wonder what these people must have thought about our relationship. They were too polite to ask if anything was wrong. I wish they would have. Knowing what I do now.

One of his major goals in life seemed to be convincing me that no other man on earth would want me as a mate or a companion or a friend if *he* left me. And I, stupidly, believed him. After what I've gone through, I'm still afraid to get involved with men. They tell me that that fear dissipates with time. My abuser had my number. He knew I feared loneliness more than anything. So I stayed with him, believing his constant claim that nobody else would want someone like me. Wasn't I lucky?

There were a few times when I actually found the strength to attempt to leave him. I moved in with my sister for a couple of weeks. Another time it was with a girlfriend.

His threats to commit suicide brought me back. He would call me up on the phone and cry, and sound desperate, claiming he could not live without me. Like a fool, I believed him. He said he loved me. That he would change. So I went back. Back to the abuse.

It wasn't until some time later, after counseling by an abuse center staff, that I learned that most batterers try this "suicide" stunt—as an emotional attempt to prevent their victim from leaving, or to get her back.

It is really true that these men are overly jealous and want to retain control of their mates. They just don't want any other man to have them. It's a jealousy thing. A male thing. It's as simple and as complex as that. I don't really understand it. But I know that my mate was that way. He could have his other women, but there was no way he'd ever let another man as much as look at me without getting violently jealous and insecure. He was too stupid to see that he was the only man I wanted. If only he had treated me nice.

There were times when he did treat me nice. Those times were wonderful. He brought me flowers. He took me out to dinner. He was a master at acting and talking lovingly—when he wanted something from me. Or even when he knew I was fed up to the point where I was about to leave him. So I stayed. For a while.

The insecure atmosphere he created around us was unnerving. All those times when he did not come home from work on time. I'd sit up worrying that he'd been hurt on the job, or was out on a drinking binge with his buddies (and might come home and abuse me), or was with some other woman, or in a pornography store viewing obscene films. He never told me where he'd be when he pulled these tricks to unsettle me. Yet when he'd get home late, I'd get accused of not keeping dinner warm for him, or be lectured because the food was dried out.

I know this sounds crazy. I sound crazy to have tolerated this. I know now I was not alone in putting up with such abuse from my man. Thousands, perhaps millions, of women in our nation experience similar emotional abuse from their mates every year. I think that's tragic.

Now that I've recovered, I'd like to find some way to help these other women to end their abuse.

The belief I had that he was cheating on me—sexually—was one of the most devastating aspects of his emotional abuse. When I married him, I meant it when I pledged to be faithful. I expected him to be the same way. Nobody can convince me that infidelity doesn't destroy relationships. It devastated me. There were a couple of times when I caught him talking to other women on the phone, and I realized he really had been fooling around. I got very depressed and felt worthless because of this. He, of course, denied it. But I knew he was lying to me.

He always accused me of being unfaithful to him. He was obsessed with the belief that I was sleeping with his best friend, and, later, with one of his coworkers from the office. This was all in his imagination. But try convincing a batterer of that. He was insanely jealous. For no reason. That was the strange part. I hadn't done anything wrong. He just thought I had.

His jealousy, his insecurity, his lack of trust in me, caused him to isolate me. I was emotionally devastated by the lack of contact with my family, my friends, and other human beings.

Of course, this made me much more dependent on him. Which is precisely what he wanted. I know that now. I didn't recognize what was happening to me at the time.

The financial control he exerted over me was one of the worst aspects of his emotional abuse. I had to ask him for every penny for food, for clothing, for the kids, even for personal items. This all had to be accounted for. During the times when I was not working, we were totally dependent on his paycheck to survive. And when I finally did work, part-time, I didn't bring in enough money to survive on my own. Besides, he always controlled my paycheck, too. So that was one of the main reasons I stayed with him.

I was too insecure to seek better work. Besides, I had children to care for. He wouldn't share *that* responsibility. He used to make me beg him for money. That was so demeaning. It caused me a great deal of stress and insecurity. It destroyed my options. Kept me beholden to him. He was the type of a guy who would quit his job if I left him—just to avoid having to make child support payments. At least he had me convinced of this.

He used to terrorize me by threatening to walk off with our children, or to get custody of them—if I left him. He had an elaborate scheme concocted to convince the authorities that I was a bad mother. Like an idiot I believed that he would actually fight for custody of kids he never wanted responsibility for in the first place, and that the courts would be unjust enough to give him custody of children who loved me and hated him. He had my mind so mixed up that I believed just about anything he told me.

The impact of his emotional abuse was to make me helpless to help myself, and more tolerant of his abuse.

I had lasting bouts with depression, insecurity, unhappiness, physical health problems caused by the physical and emotional abuse, and a truly negative attitude toward life.

I have put that behind me now. I am moving forward with my life, have gained self-esteem, have developed a positive attitude, and am even finding that I may be able to, someday, trust another man. One who is not abusive like my husband was. My children are doing much better, emotionally, as well.

As I reflect back on my experiences as a battered wife, I recognize that the consequences of domestic violence are so tragic, so far-reaching, and so life-threatening, as well as so emotionally devastating, that our society must make every effort within its power to prevent and end such abuse.

I ended my abuse.

And I am so very glad.

(Note to the reader: The foregoing description of the types of emotional abuse domestically abused women experience was written in the first person to take the reader into the minds of such women. The story told is the author's fictitious rendition of what such experiences are like for such women, and is not based upon any specific victim's experiences.)

Living With An Abusive Mate

Abuse is like being imprisoned in your own home due to circumstances not of your own making with no chance of escape or parole.

It is a feeling of helplessness and hopelessness that won't go away.

Like being in a cell of isolation and dependent on an abusive person for survival.

You *fear* the man who has done such ugly things to you.

At the same time you love him.

And cannot even imagine life without him.

Many times you are afraid to make decisions, to take actions, out of fear that he will become angry toward you over what you have done (or failed to do). Yet there is no real predictability about what behavior or words you speak that is likely to result in his physical aggression or emotional abuse toward you or your children.

You, in your lack of self-esteem, and learned helplessness, tolerate the most vicious, cruel, dangerous, and demeaning physical and emotional acts toward you by the abuser. These include:

—Demeaning comments about your work-related skills and abilities until you actually begin to believe you are as worthless as he claims.

—Physical batteries (inflicted by hands, feet, objects).

—Sexual batteries (rape; beatings; threatened acts; painful or demeaning sex acts; attempts to make one engage in acts one does not want to do; taking of pornographic photos which can be used to blackmail you; being forced to look at pornography or listen to humiliating or disgusting sexual fantasies).

—Isolation from family and friends.

—Actions to make certain that you cannot find or perform work (and financially support yourself).

—Causing you great emotional pain and instability by taking professional credit for *your* hard work.

—Sleeping with other women (and making certain you know about some of these acts of infidelity), while manipulating your emotions in ways which cause you to tolerate such abuse.

—Cheating you out of professional job opportunities.

—Treating you like a whore or suggesting you become one.

—Praising or cutting down your physical image and/or sexual abilities, depending on the desired manipulative intent of the time.

—Keeping you on an emotional roller-coaster with serious bouts of depression alternating with bouts of happiness.

—Making sure there are lots of times when you are unaware of his whereabouts, and being unreliable about when he'll be home.

—Using *your* financial resources to *his* advantage.

—Making certain you are emotionally and financially *dependent* on him.

—Using psychological tricks to constantly get you to agree to do things *his* way, thus taking away your ability to make choices in your life.

—Misleading you about his background and experiences in order to make you think highly of him.

—Refusing to make a marital or serious commitment to you (causing great instability and emotional pain because you want this sort of commitment).

—Trying to force you to abort the child you and he conceived by threatening to or leaving you, promising to marry you and have other kids if you abort this one, and other psychological tricks. He is selfish and does not share your value for life.

—Making you give birth to the baby without being there at your side to lend support.

—Dumping you for someone with money and position (yet expecting you to be available if he decides to come back).

—In some cases, abusing your children physically or sexually.

—Making certain you are living under conditions that make you seriously unhappy and despondent.

—Refusing to let you participate in his activities (professional or personal) which you rightfully should be involved in.

—Committing criminal acts (such as shoplifting) in front of you which he knows greatly upset you and go against your concept of right and wrong and morality.

—Threatening to and/or trying to kill you.

—Making you live in constant fear of being abused by him.

You, as a battered woman, feel *empty inside* during so much of the relationship, yet you fear you'll feel so much more empty if you leave this man or he leaves you. And so you tolerate the abuse and bury the pain of the abuse deep within. You may have been conditioned to accept abuse as a child and your abusive mate may be taking advantage of this, knowingly.

You *blame yourself* for the abuse.

You feel you deserve the abuse.

You are so ashamed of the abuse that you don't even tell your friends (if you have any left) about it—and actively cover up physical bruises and emotional scars.

You may or may not report the abuse to authorities and may or may not cooperate in efforts to end the abuse and to hold the abuser responsible in a court of law for battering, sexually assaulting, or endangering you. How you respond is highly dependent upon how the person or persons who try to help you treat you, and on whether the system acts appropriately in your behalf. The attitudes these helpers portray toward you, and even the physical surroundings of the place where you receive help, and its atmosphere, are so critical in influencing you to end or tolerate an abusive relationship.

The terror you live with day by day in your home is indescribable.

You want it to end.

You want the pain (physical and emotional) to cease.

Yet you do not want to lose him.

Or you cannot figure out a way to survive, financially, without him. The system does not provide much help to enable you to do so.

Maybe he won't leave you alone even if you take legal actions against him.

And so, the fear continues. . . .

All you really want is a chance for a fresh start, the chance to practice your profession, the opportunity to financially and physically care and provide for your child, and the right to find a safe, moral, happy, healthy personal life.

If you have recovered from the abuse enough to recognize you want those things, you may find the strength to actively seek them, and perhaps even recall the words of Golda Meir:

> If you don't believe in miracles, you're just not a realist.

CONCLUSION

The above segment was written by this author from a standpoint of taking the reader into the thought patterns experienced by battered women. The statements presented are fictitious, in that they did not occur to any specific battered woman. However, they utilize the sorts of experiences and attitudes battered women tend to have.

Perhaps as we fight abuse of persons in our society we should be in the business of looking for miracles. Or maybe each of us just has to use our talents to help other people in whatever ways we, individually, and collectively, can.

Chapter 4

WHAT IS "LOVE"?

To understand the emotional trauma caused by mate abuse, we must envision how it would feel to be physically hurt by a loved one. To do this, we must define the concept of love. Secondarily, we must examine differing ideas that women and men have about what "love" is and how those conflicts impact upon intimate relationships.

What Is "Love"?

Love is a friendship which progresses beyond—into physical intimacy.

Love involves caring, living together, wanting to be with the other person.

Love involves sharing life's good and bad occurrences, life's ups and downs, and life's responsibilities like having and raising children, financing the home and family, and working together on the day-to-day tasks of home upkeep and family care.

Love involves sharing one's intimate feelings about life, family, relationships, goals, the world, work, friends, church, health, etc. It does not involve refusing or failing to communicate genuine feelings.

Love involves trusting the loved one—completely. And not violating that trust by being unfaithful or by abusing the other person.

"Love" was described in the *Bible* (called "charity" in the King James Version) in 1 Corinthians, Chapter 13. Parts of the chapter describe how even if a person can prophecy, speak in language of men and angels, has all knowledge, has faith strong enough to move mountains, and gives all of her or his goods to feed the poor, he or she is "nothing" if he or she does not have love (charity). It reads, in part:

4 Charity suffereth long, *and* is kind; charity envieth not; charity vaunteth not itself, is not puffed up,

5 Doth not behave itself unseemly, seeketh not her own, is not easily provoked, thinketh no evil;

6 Rejoiceth not in inequity, but rejoiceth in the truth;

25

7 Beareth all things, believeth all things, hopeth all things, endureth all things.

8 Charity never faileth. . . .

13 And now abideth faith, hope, charity, these three, but the greatest of these is charity.

The concept of love set forth in the above quotes from the *Bible* is the one many people, especially women, have of the way intimate "love" relationships should be. The fact that many intimate relationships do not practice this concept of love has to come as a great shock to the women and men who are looking for that sort of commitment from their mate.

Men, Women, and Love

The author is convinced that one of the major causes of the breakup of intimate relationships (and of families) is a serious difference in how many women and men conceptualize "love."

For too many men, "love" means nothing more than engaging in sex with a woman.

These types of men do not feel, or, perhaps more accurately stated, *refuse to let themselves feel* an emotional bonding to the woman. Such bonding is necessary for long-lasting, successful relationships.

A man who cannot or will not bond emotionally to the woman he marries or lives with is likely to be unfaithful and to believe there is nothing wrong with infidelity.

Most women, conversely, consider the emotional bond with their mate to be of major importance. Many women find that they have to be emotionally in "love" with a man before they will become sexually intimate with him. Unless the emotional attraction exists for such women, the physical attraction does not develop. Many men, on the other hand, often develop physical attractions toward women without having an emotional attachment.

Ironically, it is the very fact that women develop such strong emotional bonds to their mates which makes it so very hard for them to leave abusive men.

Women also have to be concerned about realistic aspects of becoming intimate with men, including possible pregnancy or abortion, AIDS, sexually transmitted diseases, child-bearing/rearing, financial security, and home responsibilities.

In American society, some men appear to be untroubled by deserting the women they engage in sex acts with, even if children and/or financial duties are involved. As a result of our society's allowing men to escape childrearing and financial responsibilities, the potential problems facing a woman who becomes intimate with a man are so much greater than the potential problems the man faces. For her, therefore, there is frequently no such thing as a "one night stand." Many women consider these realistic aspects of intimacy before becoming involved.

Conflicting Sexual Expectations

It is important, for relationships to last, and for both parties to be happy and content, that couples have good, *mutually fulfilling* intimate relationships. Some of the stress, and some of the dissatisfaction in sexually intimate relationships may be caused by conflicting sexual expectations. The topic is so sensitive that many couples may be failing to discuss their attitudes about sex and are, therefore, unaware of the desires and expectations of their partner.

For some people, sexual activity is very important, and for others it is not.

While generalisms probably should not be made, it appears as if men in our society tend to consider sexual activity to be a major part of their lives, whereas some women share that attitude and others consider such activity to be an unsatisfactory nuisance, something unpleasant that they would prefer to avoid. Obviously the individual attitudes of people in this regard are formed by their own personal sexual experiences and the success or failure of their intimate involvement with their mates.

However, it should be mentioned that among the reasons for some women disliking sexual involvement are the failure of men to do the following:

1. Take time and care to arouse women by holding and cuddling and talking in a loving manner to them.

2. Care whether their partner is fulfilled during the sexual activity.

3. Provide the emotional love and bonding that women tend to need from their mates in order to have a successful intimate relationship.

4. Learn how to satisfy their mates and take the time to do so.

5. Accept responsibility for any consequences of engaging in sexual activity (such as pregnancy, health problems).

Clearly, there are a lot of couples who do have mutually satisfying intimate relationships. These are the sorts of relationships which seem more likely to be lasting ones.

This author argued in her book, *Sourcebook On Pornography* (Lexington, Massachusetts: Lexington Books, 1989), that part of the dissatisfaction in relationships is created by American society's promotion of infidelity, sex with strangers (and without commitment), frequent and bizarre sexual encounters, and a false "Playboy"/"Penthouse" "Bunny"/"Pet" image of how women should look, dress, act, and be physically shaped. The reality is that even the women who fit the male "Playboy" bunny or "Penthouse" pet image cannot keep a man faithful in today's society because the pornographic lifestyle promotes lack of commitment and moving from playmate to playmate, from pet to pet, instead of recognizing women as intelligent human beings. Men who buy into the pornographic concepts also tend to attempt to follow those lifestyles.

Part of the problem of dissatisfaction in intimate relationships is that many men want and expect their mates to do sexual acts which pornography convinces them are exciting, arousing, and interesting. It has to be a major letdown to their egos to discover that *real* women are not interested in doing sexual acts which are physically harmful or painful or which they personally consider nonarousing, humiliating, or degrading. Those acts are the standard fare of pornography. They include:

—Sex with objects or animals
—Anal sex
—Oral sex
—Group sex
—Sex with persons of the same sex
—Bondage/discipline/sadomasochistic acts
—Imitating acts from pornography
—Posing for pornographic/sexually explicit photographs

Obviously it must be noted that some people enjoy and are comfortable, in their lifestyles, with acts like oral or anal sex, and homosexuality or lesbianism. It is not the intent of this book to cut down, in any way, those lifestyles or sexual acts. The concern of this author is with any form of sexual activity which is not a willing choice of one of the participants in the act. The reality is that many women do not enjoy or wish to participate in the sorts of acts listed above. It is therefore wrong for their mates to force or insist that they engage in such activity. Those acts become part of the domestic abuse experienced by victims of such abuse.

Abusive men tend to become convinced that abusive sexual acts are something they want to experience and to insist their mates participate in. When the women refuse to cooperate, these men either damage the relationship by *forcing* (by physical or psychological persuasion) the women to do the unwanted acts, or they damage the relationship by finding another woman or women who will do such acts. Either outcome does great damage to the woman's trust of the man, and plays a role in the eventual destruction of the relationship.

One major part of fighting abuse has to be a strong attack on the false and destructive concepts of human sexuality which are being promoted in our society.

Sexual abuse in domestic relationships is a frequently overlooked or ignored aspect of domestic abuse. The reality is that most domestic violence victims have also been sexually assaulted and/or sexually abused by their mates. We need to start asking victims of domestic abuse questions about their sexual abuse. The fact is that the sexual abuse is one of the most terrifying, controlling, and humiliating parts of a battered woman's relationship with her abuser. The sexual abuse may, in fact, be taking place far more frequently than other forms of battery in these abusive relationships. Victims of domestic abuse usually fail to tell professionals who are helping them, and to tell friends/relatives about the sexual aspects of their abuse. It is important, therefore, that we train professionals in how to ask victims about this sensitive topic in appropriate and sensitive ways. It is critical that professionals explore the sexual abuse aspects of domestic abuse cases because ending the nonsexual physical violence by batterers will not necessarily end the sexual abuse aspects of the victimization—unless this topic is addressed and resolved in individual cases.

Can We Create Love and Keep These Couples Together?

The author poses this question to the professionals who work with the victims and perpetrators of domestic abuse:

Can We Create Love and Keep These Couples Together?

The fundamental criminal justice system issue we face, when considering response to domestic abuse cases, is whether we should emphasize ending abusive relationships, or focus on attempting to end the abuse by persuading abusers to think and behave in a genuinely "loving" manner toward their mates.

If we do not begin to put aside the dogmatic, irrational, uncompromising thinking, teaching, and actions of the radical feminists regarding abuse, and to put aside the equally dogmatic, irrational, uncompromising attitudes and behavior of the radical right religious conservatives, we, as a society, are not going to solve the abuse problem. It is as irrational to keep separating abusive mates without changing abusive behavior as it is to encourage persons who are abused to remain with their abusers and to tolerate the abuse.

When you, as a professional, or when you, as a friend, relative, neighbor, coworker, face a woman who has been domestically beaten, sexually assaulted, or otherwise abused, you are likely to be dealing with someone who has a heartfelt emotional (love) attachment to the man who abused her.

She has been devastated by the fact that someone whom she loves and trusts and wants to spend her life with has hurt her physically, sexually, and emotionally.

Because she instinctively knows it is not "loving" to physically batter someone, to sexually abuse someone, or to emotionally terrorize a person.

If we take someone who has a concept of love similar to that set forth in the excerpts from the *Bible* quoted earlier in this chapter—one that rejoices in truth (honesty, trust?), believes and hopes and endures all things, thinks good, not evil thoughts, is kind, and tolerant, and caring— and we expose her to abuse from the man she loves, it has to be a terrible shock which is next to impossible for her to handle, emotionally.

The faith (in God's goodness and protection and help), the hope (part of the human way of thinking), the tolerance, the "love" she feels in her heart for the batterer, helps prevent battered women from ending abusive relationships, persuades them that things will get better, that he will change (because he "loves" her)—and none of these hopeful opinions are necessarily true. And that has to scare abused women. It must terrify them, in fact.

Genuine love of the type described in the *Bible* (which can be applied to both intimate love and the sort of love human beings are supposed to have toward each other), is a beautiful, healthy, wonderful concept. We can't blame anyone for seeking or expecting that sort of love in their personal lives.

Ironically, it is the genuine feeling of such love, and the desire for such love from one's mate, that keeps battered women in abusive relationships.

The failure of abusive men to share such concepts of love is a serious hindrance to successful continuance of such relationships.

Professionals, therefore, find themselves faced with battered women who cannot come to grips with the reality of the abuse, and who often continue, precisely because they "love" the abuser, to attempt to make things better. The women do not know that the abuse will get worse unless the abuser changes the attitudes in his own heart and makes corresponding behavioral changes. If we were to tell the women this, many will not believe us.

When we consider trying to keep these couples together, the issue becomes whether we can honestly expect to change the batterers' behavior and attitudes to make them both behave and think lovingly toward their mates. If we can do this, it is probably worth attempting to preserve some of these relationships for the sake of family stability. If we cannot do so, our only reasonable actions, as professionals, must be to encourage these women to take legal steps to keep their abusive mates away from them.

This author firmly believes that the behavior and beliefs of *some* batterers *can* be altered and that we, as professionals working in this field, and we, as a society which cares about its people, and its future, *must* devote so much more time, effort, money, and dedication to attempting to do this. It is a big effort. Yet, we owe it to ourselves, and to our children, to try to end the abuse.

Falling Out of Love

As a woman who has ended her own abusive relationship, and as a professional who has helped other victims of domestic abuse, the author is convinced that the most important reason why women stay with their abusers and sometimes refuse to cooperate with police, prosecutor, and other professionals who are trying to help them end the abuse, is because they "love" the man.

This has to sound strange to persons who have not experienced this "love."

Perhaps, in some cases, it is almost like an obsessive-compulsive love interest in which the fear of losing the man is so much more frightening than the fear of the abuse to which one has become conditioned. We know this kind of thinking is not logical. Yet victims of domestic abuse tend to think that way. Until the abuse gets so severe or so frightening or so life-threatening that the victim realizes she has to end it or risk losing her life or killing the abuser.

It's an unrealistic, foolish way of thinking, this "love" conquers all concept, isn't it? Except to those who believe in it. Is it just wishful thinking? Maybe not. Maybe it's just a recognition that intimate relationships should involve love, caring, sharing, and emotional bonding. That's not foolish or unrealistic, is it? The only foolish part is for a victim of domestic abuse to think that the abuse will end without some sort of steps being taken to reform the abuser's attitudes and behavior.

The fear of loneliness, the belief that one is unable to help oneself, the dependency on the abuser (his having managed to isolate the victim from friends, family, jobs, etc.), the fear of being rejected, is so overwhelming that even the abuse seems tolerable.

Victims think about the many times when their abusive mates were affectionate, loving, nice, caring, and reliable. Those good times get elevated in their memories, and the bad times get buried deep within their subconscious, and sometimes forgotten altogether. Such distancing techniques enable the women to continue to tolerate the abuse.

Can we truly blame these women for wanting the good times with their mate to happen again?

Of course we can't.

This author is convinced that the "love," the deep, abiding, heartfelt, sincere, "love" and affection a woman feels for her abusive mate, *has to die in the woman's heart before she can take steps to effectively keep the abuser out of her life.*

Let's say it again, because this is a major point:

THE LOVE A WOMAN FEELS FOR HER ABUSIVE MATE HAS TO DIE IN THE WOMAN'S HEART BEFORE SHE CAN TAKE STEPS TO EFFECTIVELY KEEP THE ABUSER OUT OF HER LIFE.

A woman, reading this book, who has been abused, who is in love with her abusive mate, may ask whether the love she feels for him can ever truly die.

Love does indeed end. It has ended in many relationships. So we can assure the women who are currently involved in abusive relationships that the love they feel for their abuser can truly end. In fact, it has to end in order for her to be able to make the physical and emotional split from the abusive mate. If it has not ended, she is at great risk of going back to the abusive man and continuing to tolerate his abuse. Ending the love is part of ending the dependency.

Ending the love may sound like an impossible task. It isn't.

Sometimes it comes about as part of the natural progression of the bad relationship. In other words, for how long, psychologically, and emotionally, can a person continue to love or feel affection toward a mate who has battered, sexually abused, ridiculed, isolated, verbally attacked, emotionally devastated, and destroyed one's inner soul? A victim of such abuse may wake up one morning with her psychological and emotional self-defense mechanisms suddenly activated and say, enough is enough.

There has to be something better, a better way of life, than living with someone who is abusive.

A victim may suddenly realize that her abusive mate does not love her. While that is devastating, it is part of the realistic process of recognizing that the relationship is on the skids and is about to sink unless something effective gets done to repair it.

Maybe ending the love will result from a victim's exposing herself to the various helpful groups and individuals who are out there in the community willing and able to work with her to deal with the abusive relationship. If she gets her own self-esteem back, and her attitudes progressing along a sensible, realistic way of thinking, the love may begin to fade.

If the victim is able to end the isolation her abuser has trapped her in, and to begin to make friends, and communicate with relatives, and with professionals, and to build some sort of a life for herself separate and apart from the abuser, thus ending her dependency on him, her obsessive love for and dependence on him may end.

If a victim makes a conscious effort to look around her in the community, and sees people who actually are experiencing mutual love and affection, she may recognize that her relationship with her abusive mate is not like that. Perhaps she will recognize that she must either do something to create mutual love and affection in her own intimate relationship with her mate—or end the abusive relationship and move on with her life to seek and find a mate who is capable of providing mutual love and affection.

It is hard to tell a person who is caught up in a relationship with a mate, a person who is deeply in love with that mate, even though he abuses her, that she has to stop loving him or find some way, with professional help, to get the mate to start loving her and to alter his abusive attitudes and behavior.

That's the reality of abusive relationships. The abuse will continue unless something effective is done to stop it.

We, as professionals, can tell a woman who has been abused that it is irrational to "love" someone who has battered her, sexually abused her, emotionally destroyed her soul.

But we should also tell her that we understand that the love for the abuser has to die in her heart before she can effectively find the emotional strength and courage to keep the abuser out of her life.

Chapter 5

DOMESTIC ABUSERS

If we are to have, as a society, any realistic hope of preventing and ending domestic violence in the lives of millions of our people, we must take a realistic look at the characteristics and behavior patterns of domestic batterers and other abusers. Our goal must be to prevent and to alter such abusive behavior by men.

The underlying problem is that we raise our boys and men to believe that physical aggression is an appropriate way to resolve disputes. In other words, not only is physical force an acceptable part of the culture of many American males, it is actually the *expected* response. Add to that the still common attitude that men are to control women and that women are to be submissive to men, more specifically, to their husband or mate, founded in religious misinterpretation and in paternalistic traditions, and we find ourselves facing a need to make major changes in long-held attitudes in our culture. Reality suggests that true love is possible only if equality exists between partners in an intimate relationship. We must, as a nation, strive to promote such equality.

If You Were A Batterer

Suppose you were a batterer who had given his wife a black eye and made her shoulder black and blue by punching her. You also forced her to submit to painful and humiliating sexual acts against her will. This was not the first time you had beaten or raped her.

This time your wife called the police. The police took photographs of her bruises and got a signed statement about the abuse, including the past abuse history, from her.

You denied the abuse.

The police arrest you and take you to jail to be booked for battery and sexual assault of your wife.

You'd be scared about having been caught.

The fact that you had experienced a loss of control over your liberty, over yourself (by the arrest), would bother you immensely. (You are the type of man who is accustomed to controlling the liberty of your wife. Now, for the first time, perhaps, you are learning what that loss of control over self feels like. And you don't like it one bit.)

You worry about what the criminal justice system might do to you.

Will you get a criminal record as a result of this incident?

Will you have to spend time in jail?

Will the case hit the newspapers and damage your image in the community? Or, at a minimum, tell the world, your world of family, friends, coworkers, the type of person you really are? After all the effort you went through, including threatening your wife, to make certain that your abuse of her never saw the light of day.

You are very angry toward her for reporting you to the police.

Will the police, the prosecutor, the other people in the legal system, actually try to hold you accountable for the abuse and help your wife to end the abuse?

You might be intimidated into stopping your abusive behavior toward your wife if you were charged with and found guilty of battery or of endangering her life. Because you're smart enough to know that if they hit you hard for your first "reported" offense, they'll get you again if you hurt her again. You will have learned that neither your wife, nor the legal system will tolerate your abusive behavior. Stopping the abusive behavior could become a self-preservation matter for you. Besides, you and your wife got along better before you started to abuse her. And you, deep in your heart, don't want to lose her.

The problem is you don't know how to control your temper, your anger, your moodiness, your tendency to strike out, physically, at the most vulnerable person in your life—your wife. Your intentions to change may be well-meaning. Until you suddenly fly out of control again.

It occurs to you that maybe you ought to tell somebody about this. About your inability to control your violent behavior and the attitudes within you which lead to such outbursts toward your mate.

The police and prosecutors have suggested that there may be help out there for you. And boldly said that unless you get such help you're not likely to change. Who are they to know?

Yet, it might be worth looking into. To avoid another hassle with the law just like this one. They said that the next time they'll hit you with more serious criminal charges and lock you up in jail for a long time.

You don't know if they are serious or not, but it's not the kind of gamble you want to take.

You start thinking about the possibility of looking into the local batterers program. If you don't like it you can always leave.

Suppose, instead, that you, the batterer, got arrested for beating and sexually assaulting your wife, but you were not charged with a crime by the prosecutor's office.

You would believe your conduct was acceptable to society.

You would realize you could probably batter your wife again—and get away with it. You would already have gotten away with it once.

You'd be unlikely to admit or come to grips with the fact that your behavior was wrong. Hadn't men, after all, been treating their women as chattel property down through the centuries? Why should you be any different? Society hadn't changed all that much in its attitudes toward wife abuse.

You would figure that your wife's word about the abuse either was not believed by the prosecutor or that her abuse, even the evidence of physical bruises, was not important to him or her.

You would know your wife would be most unlikely to report the abuse in the future. The system had already failed to help her.

You would be very angry at your wife for reporting the abuse, for causing this hassle, for making you worry about what the system might do to you.

Under those circumstances, when the system failed to help her, you would feel safer punishing her by abusing her again.

You do not know, you would not care, that your domestic violence toward your wife will follow a pattern of escalating frequency and severity.

And you do not know that the criminal justice system just failed you both. It encouraged you to continue your abusive behavior instead of forcing you to consider changing it. And it left your wife vulnerable to your future abuse.

You think it's for the best.

But if you really think about it, is it? Will it make your relationship with your wife better?

(Author's note. The above passage is the author's fictitious account of how a typical batterer might react to various actions by the criminal justice system concerning his abuse of his wife. The information was presented as such to introduce the reader to the behavior patterns and attitudes of batterers and to make the reader reflect upon how the response, or lack thereof, of the criminal justice system to domestic abuse situations makes a difference in the long-run outcome of such relationships.)

How Police and Others Can Identify a Domestic Abuser

The data which follows is taken from a proposal presented by the author to the Milwaukee Police Department in December, 1991. It was part of the gender sensitivity segment of a plan to train members of the department on topics of cultural and social group diversity/sensitivity.

This information should be combined by professionals with the earlier parts of this book which describe the characteristics and behavior of abused women in helping determine whether a particular case involves a woman who suffers from the Battered Woman syndrome. The characteristics of a battered woman must be present in the woman, and the characteristics of a batterer must be present in the man, in order for a woman to be diagnosed as having the syndrome.

Batterers tend to have certain characteristics which distinguish them from nonabusive, nonassaultive males. This is not to state that all batterers have all of these characteristics or that nonabusive males have none of these characteristics. The presence, however, of a number of these factors in the behavior pattern of a male toward his mate can help police (and others) determine that a domestic abuse situation exists, thus allowing them to respond accordingly.

Batterer Characteristics

1. *Low self-esteem*

Batterers tend to have low self-esteem. This lack of self-esteem is a form of insecurity and certainly can impact on how the batterer treats his mate. This lack of self-worth tends to cause a batterer to want to ensure that his mate has low self-esteem as well and that she is not better than him in any way (job-wise, for example). A secure person, a person who has a positive, good self image, will, on the other hand, encourage those persons around him to have high self-esteem and to better themselves and will not be intimidated or bothered by the fact that his mate may have a better job or other opportunities that he does not have. A man with high self-esteem will consider it a positive thing for his family if his mate is successful in the work or home sphere.

2. *Dual personality*

Batterers tend to have dual personalities in which they are violent and cruel one moment and gentle and kind the next. This change of behavior, and the inability of the woman in the batterer's life to predict precisely when the batterer will exhibit one type of personality versus the other, is part of what causes the abused female's sense of insecurity and helplessness. At the same time, the ability of the batterer to be kind and loving some of the time is a major factor which keeps battered women in these abusive relationships, for it is what enables her to continue loving the man and to, unrealistically, believe that things will get better, namely, that he will change his behavior.

3. *Traditional views and the home and female sex roles*

Batterers tend to have traditional views about the home. For example, they tend to believe their mate should be responsible for things like child care and cooking and laundry, and prefer that their mate not work outside the home.

4. *Pathological jealousy and possessiveness toward their mate*

Police officers need to be keenly aware that when a male who is suspected to be a mate batterer exhibits behavior which could be described as pathological jealousy and excessive possessiveness toward the mate there is a potential for the situation to result in homicide (either the male murdering the mate or the female killing the batterer in self defense).

Examples of batterer behavior which fit in this category include:

A. Isolating the mate from family, friends, and other human contact.

B. Constantly monitoring the mate's whereabouts.

C. Suspecting the mate of having affairs with other men or women.

D. Unwillingness to let the mate end the relationship. (He may harass her, threaten to murder her, threaten to commit suicide, threaten to take the children, etc.).

5. *Pattern of controlling behaviors*

For example:

A. Threats.

B. Verbal abuse.

C. Psychological manipulation.

D. Sexual coercion/abuse.

E. Control of economic resources.

F. Undermine her.

G. Social isolation.

H. Accuse her of infidelity or family neglect.

I. Cut down her self-confidence.

6. *Blame others for their behavior*

Batterers will not accept responsibility for their abusive behavior. They tend to blame others, usually their victim, for their own behavior. For example, the batterer will claim that the mate provoked him to hit her, or made him do it.

7. *Tend to use sex as an outlet for aggression*

Many victims of domestic violence report that they experienced sexual abuse at the hands of their battering mate. Rape experiences (forcing the mate to have sex when she does not wish to have sex, or forcing her to engage in sexual acts she does not wish to engage in (for example, anal sex, sex with other persons, being bound, sex with animals, sex with objects, or being made to watch and/or imitate pornography) are reported to be common by victims of domestic violence.

8. *Have severe stress reactions*

9. *Lack concern about their violent behavior and don't believe they have short tempers*

10. *May or may not have a documented pattern of violence toward their mate or other persons*

Police who suspect someone of being a batterer should look for a pattern of abuse, but should not be surprised if they find none (for this is typically a hidden crime which goes unreported by the victim or others). In some cases, however, police may have been called to investigate abuse previously, or there may be witnesses to abuse, or there may be documentation in the form of medical (doctors, nurses, emergency room personnel) records.

Some batterers have a history of violence toward other persons outside the domestic arena. They may, for example, have knifed someone, shot someone, or have engaged in fights with other males.

11. *The public versus private behavior of batterers toward their mates and families often has dramatic differences*

The batterer may exhibit a calm, friendly demeanor when the police arrive; the battered woman is more likely to be hysterical and upset. The man may be well-respected in the community. His image with others is likely to be that of a good family man who is friendly and caring. Thus, when the woman accuses him of battering her, he may be falsely perceived by police and others as being the more credible of the two. Police must understand that this calm, friendly, respect-worthy demeanor and background is an act which the batterer is skilled at putting on for the neighbors, friends, society, and, the police. A woman who has truly been battered, however, should be expected to behave somewhat hysterically and to be upset and frightened or angry. Police must understand that battering is not more prevalent among any particular culture or age or class or level of wealth. This is not, as some falsely believe, a problem which belongs primarily to the poor classes and unemployed persons. Violent behavior on the part of males toward their mates is not something which is more common to any particular socioeconomic male subgroup. Such violence is, in fact, a widespread form of behavior among large numbers of men which continues to threaten the safety of large numbers of women in American society primarily because this issue is not being dealt with seriously enough by the criminal justice system.

12. *Minimize or deny the abuse*

Batterers often minimize or deny that the abuse occurred. They do not consider it to be a serious matter in their lives. They believe it is acceptable behavior to mistreat their mates by abusing them physically or emotionally (such as by infidelity). They may even go so far as to claim the abuse was perpetrated in self-defense.

13. *Manipulation of the children*

When there are children involved, batterers tend to manipulate their mates by manipulating the children (such as by turning the children against the mate, using visitation with them to gain access to the mate, threatening to fight for child custody, etc.).

It is important for police to understand that children whose parents or guardians are involved in a violent/battering relationship have, at a minimum, been exposed to the violence. Police must also investigate the very real possibility in mate battering cases that the children may also have been battered or, in some cases, sexually abused. Police cannot rely upon denials by the battered woman that her children have been abused, because they often lie about such abuse, choosing to cover it up, and, quite often, especially if sexual abuse is involved, are unaware that the abuse has taken place. If, for example, police have succeeded in putting a battered woman in contact with services for victims of battery (such as a shelter or counseling service), it could be quite effective to have the providers of such services be the ones to investigate the possible abuse of the children because the battered woman is more likely to be open about such matters with social worker types than police.

14. *Substance abuse*

Abuse of alcohol or drugs is common among batterers.

However, it is important for police to understand that substance abuse does not cause men to batter their mates. At most, substance abuse may serve as a disinhibiting factor, in other words, making it easier for the batterer to commit the acts of abuse. The causes, however, of domestic violence are rooted in society's acceptance and tolerance of violence, particularly in the still widespread attitudinal acceptance, especially on the part of men, of the myth that it's OK to beat one's mate. This attitude is supported by the failure of the criminal justice system in many areas, to date, to take family violence situations as seriously as they need to be taken. Many women, also, in fact, still have an attitude, which they are socialized to learn in the patriarchal society, that women deserve to be beaten or otherwise chastised or punished or controlled by the men in their lives.

15. *Resistance to changing patterns of behavior*
Batterers tend to resist changing their abusive behavior.

They often have a quick fix attitude about counseling (and may, in fact, merely play along with counseling as a way to ensure that they will continue to have legal access to their mate who might, absent counseling, leave them).

The batterers programs which appear to have the best amount of success are those which devote enough time to the batterer (over a long enough span of time) and which concentrate on teaching batterers what it is like to have their control and decision-making power taken away from them (in order for them to understand how the mates they battered feel).

Chapter 6

LETTER TO "A MAN IN POWER"

If you are a "man in power"—a district attorney, a police chief, a sheriff, a governor, a congressman, a senator, a legislator, a mayor, a city council member, a company owner/CEO, a newsman, a judge, etc. —this letter is to you.

To a Man In Power:

It Matters

It matters to me that somewhere in your community—

A woman is being battered by a mate whom she loves who is using his hands, feet, and weapons like a gun, knife, or baseball bat to seriously injure her physically and emotionally.

A child is witnessing domestic violence being committed against a beloved family member.

A battered woman, in fear of her life, will take the only step she can for self-preservation, or to save the lives of her children—that of killing her domestic abuser in self-defense while his back is turned—because our criminal justice system has failed her.

A batterer has reached the point where his anger, and frustration, and fear, and lack of self-confidence, and sadism are about to culminate in his killing his mate.

A woman is being sexually terrorized by a mate who uses the abusive practices taught by pornography to abuse her.

A child is being molested by a father while her domestically abused mother closes her eyes to the abuse.

A man has been beaten by his domestically abusive wife and is afraid to report this crime to your office or to any of the agencies which help abuse victims—out of fear of being looked down on, laughed at, or not believed.

A boy is learning to imitate the abusive behavior of his father toward

43

his mother, so that when he grows up he will commit similar acts of abuse against his mate.

A judge is refusing to sign a petition for a domestic abuse restraining order because he thinks the abuse detailed in the petition is not bad enough to justify issuing such an order.

A police officer is failing to take a woman's plea for help against her domestic abuser seriously.

A shelter is turning away a domestically-abused woman and her children because the shelter is full and has no more room.

A community of abuse-fighting professionals is failing to unite in its efforts to prevent and reduce domestic violence for the sake of preserving our families and our individual and collective physical and emotional health.

This matters, deeply, to me.

I know that you share my heartfelt concern about these matters and that you will do everything within your power as a compassionate person to fight abuse in our society. It is our duty, as responsible and caring human beings, to act to prevent such tragedy.

I know you care about this issue.

I know you are capable of a compassionate response to victims of domestic abuse.

I ask you to go beyond caring deeply about helping victims of domestic violence to taking decisive action to reduce the amount of such violence in your community.

Men in Power and Domestic Violence

This essay carries with it a certain risk.

Because you are a man in power who holds a key position which some men use to prevent anything effective from being done about domestic abuse.

Please understand that I consider you to be different than the men in power whom I describe in this letter to you. I offer these comments to you because I feel these issues are a major roadblock in our crusade to help battered women and to tackle other forms of abuse as well in our nation and state.

This letter addresses the important issue of why "we"—in other words, our society—fail to take domestic violence cases seriously. It addresses the impact of political and economic power on domestic violence.

I recognize that this is an especially sensitive aspect of domestic violence concerns.

Let me begin this philosophical essay by emphasizing that it is not intended to condemn those men in positions of power, such as you, who have chosen to depart from male customs and traditions in their thinking and behavior and to take domestic abuse situations seriously. It is meant to question, and to accuse, those men in power who still cling to concepts of paternalism and male-power which progressive and realistic men recognize as destructive and unhealthy and unwise.

I address this aspect of this issue because any serious exploration of the problem of domestic violence would be negligent if it failed to pinpoint paternalism and woman-hatred as both causes of such abuse and of our failure to do anything effective about the abuse.

In a society that fails to protect women from systematic and deliberate battery, sexual abuse, and physical and mental terrorism and torture by their mates, a society which expertly, purposefully, and pervasively condones and promotes violence against females of all ages, some women are faced with no viable way to end their abuse short of killing their abusers.

To blame those women who, in their terror, exercise that option—the only way they have to protect their bodily integrity and emotional health—is cruel, unrealistic, and unjust. Yet, when women kill their abusers in self-defense, they are typically treated like criminals by those officials (police, prosecutors, courts) who failed to take adequate steps to end their abuse on earlier occasions.

I do not believe this deliberate mistreatment by male police officers, prosecutors, and judges stems from a failure, on their part, to understand that these women did, indeed, kill in self-defense.

The root of the problem lies, instead, in the unfortunate fact that most of the men who control our courts, our governments, our police departments, our DAs offices, our businesses, our economy, and our lives subscribe to the same misogynist (woman-hating) philosophy that batterers hold dear—the idea that men should control women and that physical, sexual, and emotional abuse is an acceptable means of gaining and keeping that control. These men have more in common with, in fact, *bond* with, the men who domestically batter women, than they have sympathy or commonality with the abused women who seek their help.

Men in power perceive the issue of women effectively fighting back against domestic abuse as a power struggle between men and women. They are right in this perception. It is a struggle for equal treatment.

A woman who has acted to end her abuse, her oppression, by a man, has elected to take control of her life.

Control which is rightly hers at birth but which has been stolen from her by a society that continues to value the goals, lives, and inherent human rights (which *all* people are born with, including the right to life, liberty, and the pursuit of happiness) of men while considering female lives, goals, and rights to be relatively valueless and nonexistent.

The fact that some women have fought back against physical, sexual, and psychological terrorism by killing the men who were responsible for the abuse *terrifies* other men who hold positions of power—cops, prosecutors, lawyers, judges, jailers, probation and parole agents, etc. Especially the politicians who draft our laws to make certain that women are prevented from having and exercising equal rights.

This is true because *these* men, more than other men, know the meaning of having *control* or *power*, over other human beings. They know how to obtain such power. They know how to use that power for good or evil purposes. And they live in fear of having that power and control taken away from them.

Ironically, then, these men in power should be able to relate to how it feels to have power and control taken away from one, to relate to the powerlessness, and inability to control their own lives that all battered women experience each and every day.

Perhaps, deep down, these men of power *can* relate to this feeling of hopelessness, of complete despair. Maybe it scares them so much that they choose to block it from their minds.

These men in power dare not act to help battered women.

For, to do so would be perceived as a betrayal of their duty to perpetuate the male system of power and control of society—no matter the cost in terms of human suffering.

They do not even see that a man who thinks he has to batter a woman, or to sexually abuse a woman, or to psychologically destroy her spirit, is a man who is not in control of his own emotions, and behavior, and life.

Ironically, it was a desire to reduce human suffering that led many of the men in positions of power to seek careers as police officers, prosecutors, judges, and politicians in the first place.

They face, therefore, a strong internal conflict—between a perceived duty to perpetuate the male system of power, the old boy network, and a sincere humanistic and perhaps even a religious or social commitment to alleviate human suffering and to make society a more humane, safe, happy, and better place.

Each man in power must decide for himself which goal is more important to him. The two goals—perpetuating male power, and improving society—are in direct conflict. No compromise is possible between them.

How many of these men in power have already made the wrong choice—as evidenced by their own battering of their own mates, their infidelity, their failure to hire women for important positions in their offices, their failure to pay women equal pay for work of equal value, their sexual harassment of women, their failure to treat women as intelligent individuals rather than sex objects, and their failure to take seriously the claims of women who have been abused.

I would argue that the reason we cannot get anything effective done about domestic abuse in the United States, is because men are in control of the power spots where effective action could be taken to end the violence. Men far outnumber women in positions of political and economic power, in our courthouses, in our legislatures, in our county and local governments, in Congress, in our administrative agencies, in judgeships, in executive positions in businesses, and in other places where effective steps could be taken to stop the domestic violence.

As a result, we see:

Far more of a financial commitment by our government officials to pouring concrete and building luxurious projects than we do to increasing the funding for those aspects of nonprofit agencies, our jails, our courts, our prosecutors' offices, our police agencies, and our social service groups which help people to get back on their own two feet which relate to stopping domestic abuse.

A failure to pass effective laws to stop domestic violence. (Such as mandatory prosecution and changes in self-defense standards and expert testimony standards to realistically permit fair treatment of battered women who kill.)

A failure to enforce the laws which do exist against men who commit acts of domestic and/or sexual violence.

A failure to hold batterers accountable at the sentencing stage for their acts of violence.

The improper arrest and prosecution of battered women who kill their abusers in self-defense or while suffering from the battered women syndrome (sociological) or a psychological illness.

Battered women constantly faced with an inability to keep their batterers out of their lives because of their inability to find jobs which pay decent wages and adequate child care.

A welfare system which perpetuates dependency and poverty-level lifestyles for women and their children as part of the goal of keeping women down.

An educational system which targets men for prestigious, well-paying careers and targets women for lives as homemakers, secretaries, waitresses, nurses, and other low-paying, sex-stereotyped jobs.

Dangerous domestic batterers among the first to be released from jail when overcrowding exists.

The failure to provide enough safe places for women to go to, and enough staffs to help them draft and obtain restraining orders, and enough free legal aid to help them obtain needed divorces or custody and support orders.

A system which has no trouble understanding when a man kills someone in self-defense, but which blames the victim, a battered woman who kills in self-defense, if she takes her only way out to end the violence.

A system which fails to hire and properly utilize experts on domestic abuse to find ways to resolve individual abuse situations.

The failure to devote substantial resources to studying and taking action to change the aggressive behavior of batterers—in order to prevent and reduce the violence.

A system which never lacks dollars to arm our military or to fight on foreign soil—but which devotes only pennies in comparison to tackling problems like domestic abuse, poverty, other crime, alcohol and drug abuse, inadequate health care, poor education, and other social ills here at home.

Some religious leaders who still promote the false idea that women are to obey their husbands.

Etc.

None of this is right.

None of this is moral or just.

None of this is acceptable.

I wonder whether any of this can change absent a change in the male power elite which controls the positions of political and economic power where these changes need to be suggested and implemented.

Can you honestly say that, if women held the positions of district attorney, police chief, sheriff, mayor, a majority of the state legislature, governor, a majority in the U.S. Congress, president, chief judge (or many of these power spots)—in any given county or jurisdiction—battered women would be mistreated the way they are (ignored, not taken seriously, not helped, wrongly accused of murder, not given adequate financial support or jobs or child care or housing, etc.) at present in our society?

If your answer to that question is the same as mine is, namely, that battered women would not be mistreated the way they are now in our society, then I suppose you can agree with me that women must obtain equal power in our nation and men, including men in power, must begin to understand that a nation that wishes to survive, a nation that aspires to greatness, a nation which wants to be a world leader, and that wants to solve its social ills, must grant equal power to women in order to achieve those goals which intelligent men and women share. These are not issues which should divide humane, religious, intelligent, caring people who are committed to taking action to improve our society. We have to somehow put aside this nonsense about men and women fighting each other for control of their lives and of our society and face the fact that we all have to work together to ensure the safety, health, welfare, happiness, and survival of our children, and of ourselves. We have to share the power. And the responsibility that comes with it. For the good of all. To do anything less is to continue on the road to destruction in a nation already being undermined by the sorts of abominations warned about and preached against by the various religions.

The issue of battering another person is, therefore, more than anything else, about a battle for control of that person's physical, sexual, and emotional self.

Nobody has the right to control another person.

When our society fails to stop domestic violence, it is letting batterers control the women (and sometimes men) they abuse.

That is terribly wrong.

A Call For Action

In an interview in the February, 1993 "Focus on the Family," Bob Vernon, former assistant chief of the Los Angeles Police Department, identified four root causes of riots:

1. " . . . *the abandonment of our children.*"

2. " . . . *hedonism* —pleasure at all costs."

3. " . . . a *loss of conscience.*" (Americans "are no longer *ashamed* of wicked behavior.")

4. " . . . *neglecting principles.*" ("Political decisions are made on the basis of expediency, not principle.")

Vernon said he took these "causes" from the Book of Isaiah in the *Bible.*

It seems to me that the four items identified by Mr. Vernon apply to many of the social problems our nation faces.

Robert K. Tanenbaum, who worked in the New York County D.A.'s office, wrote a fiction novel in 1987 entitled *No Lesser Plea* (New York: Franklin Watts, Inc., 1987). The book is about a homicide case which an assistant district attorney named Karp refuses to plea bargain.

In that book, an assistant D.A., Newbury, accuses Karp of expecting the homicide bureau to be like King Arthur's Round Table. Karp denies this.

Newbury states that the bureau is composed of human beings. "Human beings are fallible, frightened and prone to corruption." He says that homicide can't survive as an elite unit "when the rest of the system is crumbling like cheese. The cops are rotten, the jails are rotten, the lower courts are rotten: it's got to touch everything—Conlin, Garrahy . . . " (Conlin is the assistant D.A. in charge of homicide; Garrahy is the district attorney.)

Karp denies that Garrahy could be gotten to. Newbury responds:

"No? There are different kinds of corruption, you know. There are sins of omission."

"What are you talking about?" (Karp)

"Look around you, damn it! The criminal justice system of this city is operated like a third-class whorehouse. It would be a scandal in Venezuala. Not enough prosecutors, not enough office or courtroom space, not enough judges, not enough jails. Police corruption? I see cops wearing clothes and driving cars I can't afford and I'm pig rich. And when was the last time you saw Garrahy making a stink about any of that on television or on the front page?" (Newbury)

Unlike the D.A. in the fiction novel, *you do speak out* against injustice and problems in the criminal justice system.

Because you are a man in power, you are listened to when you speak out.

You need to speak out—*forcefully* —on the issue of domestic violence.

You need to make it clear that domestic violence *will not be tolerated* and will be treated like any other crime against another person.

You need to *tell the truth* about the existing lack of resources to fight this important problem, and make it known that this *will not be tolerated.*

If *you* detail what is needed, the public and press (and, as a result, the politicians, decision-makers) will listen.

Why not call for:

More prosecutors and support staff.

The space needed (including interview rooms which make victims of these sensitive crimes comfortable) to properly handled domestic abuse cases.

Adequate courts to handle these cases.

Much more domestic violence shelter and center space — and more emphasis on places where victims can move to for long-term solutions.

More staff for shelters, etc.

More batterers programs and other innovative approaches.

Better networking and availability of social services, legal help, etc. to resolve abuse situations.

Why not propose and be part of a comm ttee to explore and propose innovative ways of preventing domestic violence?

If *you* identify the domestic violence arena as the DISGRACE it is, *people will listen.*

The Need to Answer Terrorism

A minister, Kenneth Copeland, gave a sermon about *Isaiah,* Chapter 54, Verse 14, on a February, 1993 television program. That verse reads: "In righteousness shalt thou be established: thou shalt be far from oppression; for thou shalt not fear: and from terror; for it shall not come near thee."

The point of Copeland's lecture was that terrorism and fear and oppression are caused by Satan, and that belief in and devotion to God will keep such problems away from people. (*Isaiah,* Chapter 54, verses 15–17.)

Copeland pointed out that people are not only to not tolerate fear, terrorism and oppression, they are to "answer it." In other words, to fight back and actively oppose terror, fear and oppression.

Domestic abusers oppress their victims.

They make these women live in a constant state of fear of physical injury and sexual abuse. Abusers *terrorize* their mates.

Don't we owe it to the victims of domestic violence to take action to end their oppression and remove the fear and terror from their lives? They may not be strong enough, alone, to do this. Isn't it *our* moral obligation to "answer" fear, oppression, and terrorism?

Chapter 7

CREDIBILITY ISSUES IN
DOMESTIC VIOLENCE CASES

The prosecutors, police, juries, judges, and social service professionals who determine the outcome of domestic abuse cases face a tremendous challenge as they weigh the credibility of the victims, perpetrators, and witnesses.

Although credibility of persons is an important factor in most court cases, it is a *major* issue in most domestic abuse cases.

The hidden nature of most domestic violence means that there will frequently be no witnesses to the abuse incidents. As a result, the credibility (or believeability) of the victim and the abuser typically becomes a key factor in deciding how to handle or what legal judgement to make in such cases.

There may or may not be *identifiable evidence* to corroborate that domestic abuse took place. The same sorts of proof problems occur in many rape and molestation cases. For example, the battery or sexual assault may or may not result in an observable or proveable physical injury.

Thus, the impression the victim and perpetrator of domestic abuse make on the case decisionmaker(s) becomes a critical factor in influencing the outcome of the case. If the victim is not very credible, or, conversely, if the abuser seems quite credible, the police may fail to arrest, a prosecutor may refuse to prosecute, or a judge or jury may fail to convict the batterer (under the tough requirement of proof beyond a reasonable doubt).

The Nature of the Abusive Relationship
Inherently Causes Victims to Lose Credibility

The behavior, demeanor, and words spoken by victims of domestic abuse is so strikingly at odds with the way the general public would expect someone who has been battered or sexually assaulted to behave, that typical jurors will find victims lacking in credibility—unless that behavior and attitude is explained to them by domestic abuse experts. Such expert testimony is not likely to be offered or available in most domestic abuse battery cases which wind up going to trial. Therefore, a smart, system-abusing, cunning batterer, knows that he will probably be able to cop a lesser plea because the prosecutor will probably want to avoid going to trial (unless the physical evidence of abuse is overwhelming or there are credible witnesses to the abuse). The rotten system is, in effect, letting domestic abusers run the show.

We don't give that sort of power to most other criminals. Why give it to batterers? That's not justice. It's expediency.

How can we expect young people who are growing up today to respect us and respect the legal system, and obey the law when we don't insist that the system become fair, and court case outcomes be just?

Among the types of illogical attitudes and behavior of domestic abuse victims are these:

1. The fact that victims *tolerate* the most extreme and bizarre types of abuse.

2. The fact that the victim often still "loves" the batterer.

3. The failure of the abuse victim to leave the relationship, to end the relationship.

4. The question of why the victim didn't report the abuse *if* the abuse was as bad as she claims.

5. The appearance that the abuse victim consented to the battery (despite the fact that some state laws do not make consent a defense to the crime of domestic battery or the lack of consent an element of the crime). (See below for section on consent.)

6. The abuse victim, unlike most other crime victims, considers the battery/abuse done to her to be her own fault. She thinks she did something to provoke him. She may believe she deserved to be hit. And, unfortunately, too many people in our society still think it's OK to hit one's mate. Such an attitude on a victim's part will fit right in with that traditional faulty way of thinking.

7. A victim may seem to be very down and out or very aggressively jealous or angry. Neither demeanor will make a good impression on a police officer who responds to a call for help or on a judge or jury. The lack of self-esteem is a product of suffering from the Battered Woman syndrome. The deep anger is an understandable and justifiable reaction

to the abuse which a victim may demonstrate to persons she believes are sympathetic to her plight—when she is away from the batterer and has found someone who is willing to listen. Some battered women suffer from more severe psychological disorders like the Borderline Personality Disorder or Posttraumatic Stress Disorder. A jury or judge who is unaware of the impact domestic abuse has on a victim may misinterpret signs of these disorders or a victim's strange behavior/attitudes as reasons to cause her to lack credibility.

8. Some victims who have been isolated by their abuser will be uncertain of how to act around people in the criminal justice system. This, too, may unfairly reduce their credibility.

The impact of these factors is to make it harder to successfully prosecute battery cases (if a trial is demanded). The only real solution to resolve the credibility issues which are inherent in the domestic abuse cases is to educate judges and jurors about the impact of such abuse on the behavior, attitudes, and demeanor of abuse victims so that they can consider those factors as they weigh credibility of alleged victims and abusers. It is clear that the use of domestic abuse experts as witnesses in most battery trials would be too costly and too time-consuming to the criminal justice system as it exists in many places at present. Fairness would suggest that such experts be utilized. Absent their use, we must do everything we can to train judges in understanding domestic abuse as part of their continuing legal education. We must also do what we can to educate the general public about the impact of domestic violence.

It is the suggestion of this author that communities write and design sensitively written booklets about domestic abuse and distribute them widely in places victims of domestic violence are likely to frequent—stores, police stations, social service agencies, community-based organizations, libraries, banks, courthouses, city halls, etc. The purpose of the booklets would be twofold: first, to enable victims to identify themselves as victims and to tell them where help is available and; second, to hammer home in the minds of the general public (from among which the members of juries are chosen) those factors which make victims of domestic abuse behave as they do. In addition, communities may wish to develop powerful video tapes about domestic abuse which can be duplicated with financial help from foundations and individuals and distributed widely free of charge to numerous groups and residents of the area.

We have to stop treating domestic abuse as something so terrible that it must be hidden and spoken about only in whispered voices. Giving this issue the light of day, and backing its victims with a positive, supportive network of professionals and criminal justice entities would do wonders for reducing domestic violence in any community.

Consent and Credibility

A major issue in domestic violence cases is the fact that it can be argued that, in some cases, domestic violence victims *consented* to the battery. Some states have eliminated consent as an issue or as a defense in domestic abuse cases because of the peculiar nature of consent issues in such cases.

In some domestic abuse cases it is true that the victim might be said to have consented to the battery. The reasons for this are numerous, but among the most important are these two:

1. The victim believes that the abuser was right to hit her because she thinks she did something wrong to cause him to do so; therefore, she cannot go on the witness stand and convincingly tell a judge or jury that she failed to consent to the battery.

2. Some domestic abuse victims will accept such violence and abuse toward them without objecting to it, fighting back, or reporting it (in marked contrast to the behavior of persons who have been battered by strangers). The fear, the insecurity, the dependence on the batterer, the isolation, the lack of self-esteem or self-worth, the reality of living with the abuser which makes it impossible or difficult to physically get away from him, and other factors can make battered women behave, think, and talk in ways which suggest they did indeed consent to the batteries against them.

However, it must be recognized that consent given under circumstances of the sort of fear and terror domestic abuse victims live with every day is not true consent at all. Our laws must recognize this reality, and our judges and juries must be told of this reality as they consider domestic battery cases.

Credibility and Standing of the Victim and Abuser

The *position,* or *standing,* of the victim and abuser in society, and the community can, sadly, become a credibility problem. For example, who will want to believe that a doctor, or wealthy businessman, or actor, or sports performer, or minister, etc. battered his wife or girlfriend? How can her standing as a housewife or someone who works at a less prominent job, compete (under our misguided values in society)? What if the woman has a history of alcoholism or mental health problems caused by the abuse? Conversely, the victim may be the one with a good job, and the abuser down and out and unemployed.

These emotion-laden factors are not genuinely relevant to the question of whether the abuse took place, professionals know. Yet, these are factors jurors tend to be influenced by. Do we have some sort of an obligation to see that judges instruct jurors not to consider such factors in determining someone's guilt or innocence in these cases?

Emotional Issues and Credibility

The highly-charged emotions surrounding domestic violence brings out a tendency of victims and perpetrators and witnesses to exaggerate and lie, and to express, openly, emotions like fear, anger, hurt, jealousy, and depression. This behavior creates issues of credibility.

Obviously, in cases involving family affairs, various parties may have reasons (such as to avoid arrest/prosecution, or to gain child custody) to lie to the judge/jury or professionals involved in the cases. This reality, combined with the types of emotions often displayed in such cases, makes it harder than usual for judges/juries, police and prosecutors to judge the credibility of the parties.

One aspect which makes credibility in domestic abuse cases too difficult to judge is the fact that, unlike most other criminals, domestic batterers genuinely often do not recognize that they have committed a crime or done anything wrong. They will also frequently deny having beaten their mates. Thus, these cases often do revolve around the word of one person against another person.

In those cases where someone *witnesses* the domestic abuse, the witness is typically a child, a relative, a family friend (or friend of one party to the dispute), or a neighbor. This contrasts with many other types of crimes in which witnesses are strangers with no personal interest in the case outcome. Witnesses in domestic disputes often side with the victim or the abuser. Thus, their credibility is not that of a neutral, uninvolved observer. This, too, makes it hard for decisionmakers to judge credibility in domestic abuse cases.

Credibility and Details of the Abuse

The details of the alleged battery and/or sexual abuse in domestic violence cases typically raise all sorts of credibility questions in the minds of the members of the general public because the allegations are often so bizarre as to seem unbelievable to persons who have not been victimized or who have not professionally worked with victims of abuse.

A comparison can be made to abuse cases where dozens of children claim to have been abused by day care workers or Satanists who sacrifice babies and animals, molest children, and make child pornography. I personally know victims of such child sex rings. There is good cause to believe that at least some of these cases are truthful. However, such cases often fall apart because jurors and the public simply will not accept the fact that such bizarre activities occur in the United States.

Domestic abuse often involves the type of sexual abuse and battery portrayed in pornographic films, magazines, and books. The extreme nature of this sexual abuse makes jurors, police, prosecutors, and others question whether it occurred—especially since the victim typically tolerated the abuse for a long period of time before authorities became aware of it. It does occur. Far more frequently than any of us want to acknowledge.

When women, children, or men come to professionals or their friends, family, neighbors, with such strange allegations of abuse, it is important that the person indicate that she/he believes the victim, and takes steps to convince judges and juries that such stories are, indeed, credible. This is the sort of material that people's worst nightmares are made of. Unfortunately, for many domestic abuse victims, those nightmares are their reality.

CONCLUSION

The credibility issue in domestic violence cases, therefore, becomes one of who to believe, the victim, or the abuser. To put it in the sort of terms a victim might use:

> I don't think you believed me when I told you about his abuse of me.
> I don't blame you for having doubts.
> My story sounds so bizarre.
> It's my word against his.
> He's well-known and respected in the community.
> And I'm a nobody.

Chapter 8

MAKE A RECORD OF THE
DETAILS OF THE ABUSE

When a professional evaluates or interviews a victim of domestic violence, she or he needs to take detailed notes or possibly, depending on the circumstances, consider audio-taping (or in the case of battered women who killed their abuser, video-taping) the discussion.

The details of the abuse which the professional seeks from the domestic abuse victim must be as thorough as the who, what, when, where, why, and how that journalists ask persons they interview for news stories.

The details sought should include many of the following, and certainly not be limited to those inquiries. The way the interview/evaluation is conducted, and the topics covered will, of course, vary with the facts of the particular case.

1. Name, age, address where she resides, who resides there with her, address where the abuse occurred.

2. Name, age, address, workplace, education, background of the abuser.

3. How is the abuser related to or involved with the victim.

4. When and where did the abusive incident occur?

5. Description of the abuse and facts surrounding it.

6. Have there been prior incidents of abuse? (Detail when, where, nature of the abuse, what was said, etc.)

7. Who, if anyone, was this abusive incident, and were prior abusive incidents reported to? What was the result?

8. Does the abuser have a history of violence toward anyone other than this victim?

9. What injuries occurred from the abuse (if any)?

10. Are there any medical records of the injuries from this or prior abusive incidents?

11. Was sexual abuse involved in the incident, or is it involved in the relationship in any way?

12. What words were exchanged during the incident(s)?

13. Were there any witnesses to the actual incident(s), or did anyone see her injuries?

14. Are children involved in this relationship at all?

15. What weapons (guns, knives, bats, other), if any, were used in the incident(s)?

16. Were hands or feet used to abuse the victim?

17. What is the batterer's height, weight, training in self-defense or other fighting, strength, etc.

18. How did the professionals or friends or family members whom the victim told about the abuse react to her telling them of the abuse?

19. Was the victim, or the batterer, abused as a child in any way, or the witness to abuse of any sort as a child?

20. What is the victim's work history, marital and relationship history, educational background, lifestyle, attitude toward life.

21. How does the victim feel about the abuse? (Does she blame herself or him, feel angry, depressed, afraid, betrayed, etc.)

22. What problems exist in the relationship. (Financial, emotional, infidelity, stress, etc.)

23. Did the victim try to defend herself in any way against the abuse this time or on prior occasions? What was the result?

24. Does the victim want the batterer prosecuted? Why or why not?

25. How afraid of the abuser is she? (In other words, is the situation approaching a crisis level where she or he may actually kill or severely injure the other.)

26. What support system does she have, if any? (Friends, relatives, coworkers, professionals, counselors, church, etc.)

27. Is there a history of alcohol or drug abuse on the part of either party? What, if anything, has been done about this.

28. Has the abuse been escalating in either dangerousness of the abusive acts or frequency of the acts?

29. Has there been prior contact with any social service agency regarding the abuse?

30. What sorts of services would benefit this victim. (Financial, educational, jobs, counseling, restraining orders, legal help with divorce or custody or other problems, police, medical, support group, etc.)

31. Is she safe going back to her home? Are her children safe? Does she need to go to a shelter?

32. Has she gotten a restraining order against the abuser, and should she get one if she has not?

33. How did the police treat her during their arrest of the batterer (if he was arrested)?

34. (Perhaps provide her with a video or written materials on domestic violence, or somewhere where she could go to see such information).

35. What sort of a value system does she have, compared to her abuser.

36. How does the batterer demonstrate love?

37. How does she feel about remaining with the batterer versus removing him from her life.

38. What specific options are available to this particular victim in this situation.

39. Explain how the criminal prosecution system will work and provide her with victim/witness services.

(Please note: In cases where the victim has killed the abuser in self-defense, a psychological autopsy should be done on the batterer, along the lines of that outlined by Bruce W. Ebert in my book, *Representing... Battered Women Who Kill.*

Medical Professionals and Battered Women

Medical professionals, particularly doctors, psychiatrists, and nurses, can play a critical role in detecting and ending domestic violence.

Medical professionals need to be trained in how to recognize injuries which may have resulted from domestic violence. They also need to be taught how to ask the sensitive types of questions which will be most likely to get their patients to admit injuries were caused by such abuse. One critical aspect of such inquiries will be to recognize when a patient's story of how an injury occurred does not make logical sense when compared to the nature of the injury. In any questionable case, a sensitive inquiry should be made. The vast literature on injuries resulting from child abuse should be consulted and compared to domestic abuse injuries.

It is important for medical professionals to recognize that their intervention in suspected violence cases can prevent future abuse and help abuse victims to survive and go on with their lives.

Sadly, an accurate record of physical injuries (documented by health professionals) is an important evidence base for proving self-defense claims when battered women are forced to protect themselves by killing their abuser.

Psychiatrists (as well as psychologists) need to be especially aware of the fact that a major cause of psychological problems (including stress and depression which often get treated with drugs) is domestic abuse. In order to help these patients the cause of their depression and stress must be explored so that the causes can be eliminated and medications do not become a necessary treatment for great lengths of time. The dangers of certain medications to long-term health are well-documented.

The role of medical professionals in detecting abuse is so critical, not only because such experts can document the nature, seriousness, and causes of the injuries, but also because patients tend to place a great deal of trust in the advise of such professionals. A suggestion from a doctor or a nurse regarding steps to take to end abuse may be listened to by a patient while the same advice from someone else might be disregarded.

It is important for health professionals to network with other professionals in order to know where to direct abused persons to go for help with other aspects of the abuse situation.

Police, shelter workers, and others who take abused persons to hospitals or medical clinics for treatment of injuries or documentation of sexual assaults should follow a policy of notifying the medical experts that the injuries may have resulted from domestic violence. However, it would have to be ascertained that privacy interests of the victim would not be violated by the person who releases the information.

Health professionals must be trained in how to recognize the behavioral patterns of domestic abuse victims, not just in recognizing physical injuries resulting from abuse.

It has been said that domestic abuse is the cause of many dollars worth of medical care, as well as for massive losses of work days and work productivity. Thus, society has an economic as well as a social justice purpose in reducing domestic violence. With health care costs out of control in our nation, we have an added incentive to tackle the problem of domestic abuse.

Health care professionals are so numerous. Think of the impact a massive assault by these people on the problem of domestic abuse would have!

From a prosecutor's perspective, medical/psychological records and health professional testimony can be an effective weapon in winning (or even in plea bargaining) domestic violence cases.

CONCLUSION

It is so critical for professionals to make detailed records of the domestic abuse which is either reported to them by victims of such abuse or gained as a result of their own inquiries on the topic. This detailed data is needed to help the victims determine how to resolve their domestic abuse dilemmas. It may also be needed in court in cases of battery, or murder of the batterer by the victim or of the victim by the batterer.

Chapter 9

OUT OF THE DARKNESS INTO THE LIGHT: EXPOSING THE VIOLENCE

This chapter concerns the need for victims of domestic abuse to take the critical first step of exposing their abuse to the light of day and with appropriate first responses of professionals and lay persons to victims who tell them about their abuse.

Exposing the Violence

The most important first step for victims of abuse in taking action to end their abuse is to expose their abuse to the light of day by telling somebody about it.

The most important first step to end the domestic abuse in an individual relationship is for someone (victim, friend, relative, child, witness, neighbor, co-worker, or professional) to REPORT the abuse or suspected abuse to someone who can act to do something about it (police, prosecutor, social services, an attorney, battered woman center/shelter/hotline, etc.).

Our laws require certain professionals to report suspected child abuse and in the state where this author is from, Wisconsin, elder abuse. Why not require suspected domestic abuse of adults to be reported by certain professionals who come into contact with such victims?

The truth is that female adult victims of domestic abuse are as vulnerable, and as helpless, as other victims of abuse such as the elderly and children—no matter what we, as a society, and women who are feminists would like to believe. For us to fail to recognize this fact, this helplessness and vulnerability of adult female victims of domestic abuse, is a travesty. We can't justify closing our eyes to suspected domestic abuse, and failing to report such abuse, or, if in a position to do something about it, failing to take steps to do something about it. Just because the victims involved are adult women whom our society presumes to be capable of taking care of themselves. These women are capable of taking care of themselves—once the threat to their lives, their health, and their emotional well-being, namely, the batterer, has been removed from their lives. To admit that such women are vulnerable, that they are victims, and that they need help from caring professionals, friends, neighbors, and coworkers, is not the same as saying they are unable to care for themselves or to run their own lives. It is merely saying that they need help to make their abuser alter his behavior or to remove his presence and his constant threat from their lives—and let them go on running their own lives.

How to Tell if Someone You Know is Being Abused

The general public and professionals need to be carefully taught *how to tell* if someone they know is being abused.

That is one of the reasons this author decided to write this book. To help the general public and professionals recognize victims of domestic abuse and to encourage them to take steps to end the violence.

Victims of domestic, sexual, and/or child abuse have a certain "look," an expression, a demeanor, which is recognizable to other persons who have been similarly victimized. This author is convinced that professionals and the general public can be taught to recognize that "look" in addition to being taught how to spot physical and behavioral signs of victimization.

This author attempted to describe the "look" of a battered woman in Chapter 1 in order to help persons identify such victims. Also helpful in determining whether someone you come into contact with may have been domestically abused is Chapter 3 concerning the emotional abuse such victims experience (told from their perspective). Chapter 4, about "love," may also be helpful in this regard. Chapter 8 is a blueprint for persons to use in asking suspected abuse victims about the abuse.

If I had to sum up the "look" of a domestic abuse victim in one word for people to think of in trying to determine whether they should ask a person whether she or he has been abused, it would be to state that such victims look "VULNERABLE."

The following sorts of appearances or behavior on the part of someone who may be suspected of being a victim of domestic abuse could be indicative of abuse and suggest that the belief that the person may be a victim should be explored further.

1. Noticeable out of character behavior, changes in behavior, demeanor, or appearance.

2. A "vulnerable" look.

3. Lack of self-confidence as demonstrated by behavior like the failure to look someone in the eyes, shyness, etc.

4. If the person suddenly becomes unavailable to get together with her friends for social gatherings.

5. Isolation of the person from friends, family, coworkers, social activities.

6. Onset of more illnesses and medical problems than is usual for the person.

7. Nervousness, jittery, or anxious demeanor.

8. A sad look, like that of a lost puppy; looking at her is like looking into someone's soul.

9. Depression, unhappiness, tension, suicidal tendencies or thoughts.

10. Noticeable changes in physical appearance such as weight gains or losses, palor, unhealthy appearance.

11. Bruises or other physical injuries (cuts, broken bones, burns, etc.).

12. Sleeplessness.

13. Lack of communicativeness, unresponsiveness.

14. Behavior which is overly exuberant, like the person is putting up a front, putting on an act, a pretense, especially if such behavior is not her normal demeanor.

15. Appears to get upset or sad when abuse is talked about or when reading abuse-related stories in newspaper or hearing of such happenings on TV.

16. Looks frightened in general, or seems afraid of everything.

17. There is a sudden increase in the time the woman takes off from work (unexplained by other reasons such as medical illness), or a lack of ability to concentrate, a noticeable decrease in job performance.

18. The woman gives up things which mattered a great deal to her previously, such as work, education, or other goals.

19. She does things to get attention for no logical reason.

20. The presence of disguises such as sunglasses, thick makeup, wearing of long sleeves on hot days, or otherwise inappropriate cover-up clothing.

21. A change in habits such as drinking, smoking, drug use (legal or illegal).

22. Putting on a tough-guy act as a pretence of being in control of her life.

23. Outbursts of anger toward others such as children, society, husband/mate.

24. Crying spells, and emotionalism.

25. She lets her mate run her life by letting him make decisions which would be jointly made in a relationship founded in equality—such as budgeting, spending money, etc.—and her mate seems very controlling.

26. Listlessness, inability to make even the simplest of decisions, lack of goals, appearance of helplessness.

27. Inability to trust others, suspiciousness.

28. Mate has a history of prior abuse of other women or of child abuse/neglect.

29. Sometimes loses the ability to properly care for her children and may neglect or abuse them.

30. Insecurity.

31. Pessimistic attitude toward life, feeling that she has no control over her own destiny.

32. Unusual quietness due to something other than the natural shyness some people have.

33. The mate is known to be overly possessive.

34. Looks hurt, sad, forlorn.

35. Frustration.

36. Moodiness, sudden mood swings.

37. Antisocial behavior (such as committing crimes) when this is not part of this person's usual behavior pattern.

38. Signs that she may be suffering from the battered woman syndrome, posttraumatic stress disorder, or a borderline personality disorder (described earlier in this book).

Obviously many of the behavior patterns and attitudes and demeanors described above could also be symptoms of other problems being experienced by the person in question—such as poverty, child sexual abuse, victimization, the breakup of a personal relationship, job stress or loss, etc.

However, the presence of the above sorts of attitudes or behavior could be a reason for a professional or a friend to investigate further their suspicion that their client or friend may be the victim of domestic abuse.

The Cover-Up

Professionals and lay persons who want to approach someone whom they suspect is the victim of domestic abuse to find out whether the person is indeed a victim need to understand that, even if the approach is right, the victim (99% of the time) will deny (at least at first) that any abuse took place.

Victims will blame bruises on falls down stairs. Cuts will be the result of an accident caused by the victim's own clumsiness. Makeup and dark cover-up clothing will be used to hide evidence of abuse. As will sunglasses. Sexual abuse, unless severe injury or infection requiring treatment is present, is easy to cover up.

Domestic abuse victims cover up the truth for two reasons:

First, they deny that the abuse took place as part of their own denial (refusal to accept) that a loved one could hurt them.

Second, they blame themselves for the abuse and are ashamed of and embarrassed about it.

It is not easy for professionals to get the victim past this stage of denial. What is really frustrating for people in positions to do something constructive about the abuse is the fact that victims do lie (when they deny the abuse occurred).

The reality is that most women do not even tell their best friend(s) or closest relative(s) that they are being abused.

Admitting that they were abused is the first step to recovery for victims of domestic, sexual, or child abuse. The hidden nature (it takes place in private without witnesses, usually, or with children as witnesses and is covered up by both perpetrator and victim) of domestic violence is precisely what enables it to continue unabated and worsening in so many violent relationships.

Bringing the abuse to light is the critical first step.

Inquiring About Abuse

One thing is very clear.

It does not help a situation where there may be abuse of a woman by her mate for a friend, relative, child, neighbor, coworker, or professional who suspects she may be abused to ignore that possibility.

Because ignoring this type of problem does not make it go away.

Caring professionals, friends, relatives, people should feel an obligation to make a sensitive inquiry of their friend, relative, client, or even a stranger in some cases, to find out whether the person might be being abused.

If you're wrong to suspect abuse, that's okay. It still will have been better to have inquired about it than to wake up some morning and find out that the person you thought might be an abuse victim was killed by her mate, killed her mate in self-defense, or got seriously injured by an abuser.

A word of warning. Expect the person to deny that she is being abused. If you know her maybe you can tell that she's lying. Or maybe you, as a professional, have learned how to tell when someone is not telling you the truth. Don't let it go at that. Inquire further. If you're wrong, that's good news. If you're right to suspect abuse, you will be glad to have helped the person who is being abused.

The First Responses

It is absolutely critical that whomever the victim tells about the abuse show sympathy, makes it clear that she or he believes the victim (no matter how bizarre or horrible the details of the abuse are), and indicates forcefully that he or she does not blame the victim for the abuse.

Abuse victims may be more likely to tell strangers or casual acquaintances about the abuse than they are to tell family members or close friends. Therefore, professionals and/or casual acquaintances should not be surprised if the person who tells them about the abuse has not told her family or friends.

The right type of sensitive and caring response and inquiry by a friend or professional can uncover the truth about the abuse.

It is important to emphasize that persons whom a victim tells about the abuse must not allow themselves to become part of the victim's secrecy. Something which will work to end the abuse needs to be done to help the victim. Becoming part of her cover-up solves nothing. It merely allows the abuse to continue. The person(s) whom a domestic abuse victim confides in must convince her or him to report the abuse to someone who can do something useful to stop the abuse. This person should consider going with the victim to a shelter, police, an attorney, a prosecutor, a social worker, or other appropriate resource to seek the necessary help.

Data about where help for victims of domestic violence is available should be readily available in the form of leaflets distributed throughout the community (in places like banks, stores, social service agencies, libraries, police stations, courthouses, etc.). Video tapes should also be available on this topic in today's society which is so television oriented. The materials should be written in a way that is understandable to even the poorly educated, and should be available in English and other languages where substantial populations of persons who are not English-speaking reside.

In some situations (where an injury requiring treatment or a sexual assault has occurred) the first response may include getting necessary medical treatment for the victim.

Many, if not most, domestic abuse victims have, often on a frequent basis, or at least occasionally, suffered some sort of sexual abuse as part of their abuser's terrorist acts against them. We need to take steps to recognize this fact and incorporate sexual abuse type counseling and help into our domestic abuse programs. Many men who are abusive/aggressive toward women tend to use sexual acts as a form of terrorism/control over the women.

Often, an appropriate first response to a person's statement that she has been domestically abused will be to call the police.

The Police Response

All police officers need to be *effectively* trained in appropriate handling of domestic violence cases, preferably by a team-teaching approach involving a police officer, a prosecutor, and a staff member from a domestic abuse center. Domestic violence cases will make up a disproportionate portion of the types of calls for service that police officers will be called to respond to. The training police are given in this area should be extensive and should also involve guest speakers, experts, and most certainly domestic abuse victims to tell of their abuse experiences. The training must aim to make officers sensitive to the experiences of domestic abuse victims and go beyond teaching them when and when not to make a mandatory or nonmandatory arrest. In the macho world of the police subculture, gender bias is a very real concern professionals must have as this attitude impacts not only upon the negative attitudes and behavior of the male cops toward their female colleagues, but also upon the attitude and behavior of male police officers toward female victims of domestic abuse. This is a major reason to make certain that our police departments become more diverse in their gender, ethnic, sexual orientation, racial, and other makeup.

It cannot be emphasized enough that the last thing a victim of domestic abuse needs to see on her doorstep in response to her call to police for help is a male police officer in a uniform behaving in a typically macho, authoritative manner. We need to remember that a domineering male in her own life has already hurt and/or threatened her safety and emotional well-being. The officer who responds to her need for help must be gentle, caring, sensitive, and nonthreatening. He or she must take care to make her feel secure and to establish a trust relationship with her. If the victim has to go to a police station to make a statement about the case, the police should make certain that the statement is taken in a comfortable, nonthreatening room, not in the tiny, uncomfortable rooms normally used for interrogating prisoners. Police need to keep in mind that the abuse of the woman threatens her entire emotional and financial security and that the criminal justice system is there to help her regain control over her life and her well-being, not to add to her insecurity.

Part of the police response to domestic violence victims should include providing them with telephone numbers of domestic abuse centers/shelters, prosecutors, social services, financial aid agencies, and other relevant organizations which will help them to end the abuse in their lives. In fact, the police should go so far as to offer to call a domestic abuse center or hotline for the victim of the abuse right at the scene of the abuse (if the abuser has left the scene or been arrested), and, if the victim permits, make the phone call for her. Each police officer should have spent time with the staff of such shelters/hotlines/restraining order drafting agencies and prosecutors to familiarize himself or herself with the services such groups provide to victims and to get to know the staff members who work with abuse victims. This will also be helpful to the officers as they prepare to testify in court trials involving domestic abuse battery or assault cases. The police play a very critical role in ensuring that domestic abuse victims obtain the help they need to end the abuse—by putting them in touch with appropriate agencies shortly after the abuse occurs. This is the time when the victim is most likely to become willing to seek and accept help. Police officers, more than any other group of people, are in a position to encourage and help victims of domestic violence to seek help to end the violence. They also have a self-preservation interest in seeing that such victims obtain help. Police want to avoid potential injuries in volatile domestic violence incidents. The longer a specific victim waits to get help, the more frequent and more violent the incidents of abuse against her by her abuser will become. Thus, it becomes more dangerous for police to respond to such calls for assistance. In addition, police want to avoid having to spend time being repeatedly called to the same locations and trying to continually resolve these domestic disputes. It is therefore in their interest to see that a victim of domestic abuse receives the help she truly needs at the time of her first call for police help.

Police must put aside the attitude that domestic abuse disputes are somehow considered to be less important crimes than other battery and assault cases. Regardless of whether or not the rest of the criminal justice system (prosecutors, judges, etc.) takes these cases seriously.

This author cannot emphasize enough the importance of a proper, sensitive police response to a domestic violence call. The police officer, if he or she responds sensitively to the victim, and makes it clear that he or she considers the abuser to have done a criminal/antisocial/wrong act, is likely to be seen as someone whom the victim can trust to help her. This makes it more likely that she will be willing to seek and accept help to end the abuse. An improper or insensitive response by a police officer at a scene of a domestic dispute may frighten the victim out of cooperating in criminal charges and out of seeking help from a shelter or other appropriate agency.

The domestic abuse arena is one area of policing where a proactive, or community-oriented policing approach to such cases will do much to prevent future violence/crimes and to resolve the situation. Unless we begin to use such an approach to policing, in general, we merely continue to arrest and prosecute criminals without effectively preventing new crimes from taking place.

Police failure to take domestic abuse cases seriously can, at times, result in their being sued for failing to protect domestic abuse victims. In addition, an inadequate police response, for example, failure to arrest an abuser and to put the victim in touch with appropriate services, can result in tragedy. In the battered women who kill cases this author has been involved in and in many cases I have studied, I have been repeatedly told and read that police officers were called to the scene of prior domestic disputes by the same parties and failed to adequately resolve the situation or arrest the abuser. When the police do not take adequate action, it is far less likely that the victim will seek their help the next time abuse occurs. In addition, an inadequate police response lets the batterer know that the police do not take the crime seriously and encourages the batterer to repeat the abuse. The police will have minimized the seriousness of the offense and, in effect, have justified it by their inaction. The batterer will have gotten away with the abuse and will think he can abuse the victim without threat of official intervention. In some cases this can invite more abuse as soon as the police walk out the door.

Police need to understand that victims of domestic abuse will often turn against them and side with the abuser when they make an arrest. Noncooperation of the crime victim results from several factors, the most important of which consists of the symptoms of the Battered Woman syndrome which these women suffer from. The women fear the abuser will hurt them more if they cooperate with authorities. They fear loss of the man in their lives more than they fear the abuse (due to being conditioned into learned helplessness, and dependency on the man). Jail time could cause job problems for abusers and a financial strain for the family. Arrest sometimes results in fines a family cannot afford. These fines often hurt the victim and the children. The most important reason why the women stay with the abuser and often do not cooperate with police and prosecutors is because they *love* the man.

Importantly, police must treat domestic violence against women as seriously as they treat other forms of battery and crimes against persons. To fail to do this is a form of gender discrimination and a mockery of justice.

Approaching a Victim of Domestic Abuse to Offer Help

The approach used by persons toward women who are suspected to be victims of domestic abuse will vary greatly depending upon the persons involved, their relationship, and the circumstances of the situation.

In every case, it is important that the person who offers to help develops some sort of rapport with the victim, gains her trust, and does not violate that trust.

The demeanor exhibited by the person who is trying to be helpful, whether professional, stranger, friend, family member, coworker, neighbor, is extremely important to a successful offer of help. The person who wishes to help someone whom she/he believes may be the victim of domestic abuse must exhibit a demeanor which is:

Friendly
Concerned for her well-being
Supportive
Interested in the person and what she says
Sincere
Nonthreatening
Informed about available sources of help
Helpful
Reliable
Trustworthy

Perhaps most importantly, you must portray the impression to the victim that you believe her claims of abuse and that you take her fears, problems, and situation seriously.

Because situations vary so dramatically, it is not possible to suggest any one or any set of approaches to bringing up the topic of possible domestic abuse with someone whom you suspect may be a victim. This author can only advise you to use your best judgment of what would be most effective in a given situation, keeping in mind the need to portray the type of demeanor described above. I suggest below only a handful of potential approaches in varying situations.

1. If you are a police officer, a prosecutor, or a social service person who has been put in contact with the person as a result of a report of abuse, and she already knows why you are talking to her, use a low key, nonthreatening, gentle approach to get her to open up to you about the circumstances of the abuse. Make it clear that you believe her and that you consider her to be a victim of abuse. Make sure the setting in which you talk with her is one in which she feels secure, safe, and comfortable. This author also believes that it is often appropriate to try to have someone of the same sex, culture, ethnicity, social group handle such cases so that differences of culture do not interfere with the ability of authorities to help these victims.

2. If the victim attends a lecture on abuse which you have just given as a lecturer, make certain that she, and everyone else in class, gets literature detailing where she can go for help. Invite victims to speak with you after class, or, to avoid their being singled out and noticed, invite them to phone you at a certain number during a specified period of time.

3. If the victim is a friend, neighbor, coworker, acquaintance, you might consider bringing up the abuse topic by telling her that someone else whom you know is being domestically abused by her mate, and

asking her advise on what you should tell this person to do. If you are a victim of domestic abuse, namely, an abuse survivor, you might share this information with her in order to help her to understand that she is not the only one this happens to and that it is nothing to be ashamed of or to blame herself for.

4. If you are a medical doctor or a nurse or a health professional who suspects that a patient has lied to you about how she received an injury you treated her for (i.e., black eye, broken bones, bruises, sexually transmitted disease, cuts, burns, etc.), your best approach may be to confront the victim with the fact that her story does not match the physical injuries you are treating, and ask her if she is the victim of abuse in a sensitive way.

Whatever approach you chose to use in an individual situation, it is critical that you include in your communications to the victim an offer to help her end the abuse and resolve the problems which are related to the abuse (such as by going with her to see appropriate authorities, social services, an attorney, etc.). At a time like this, the victim needs to know that she will have at least one support person beside her as she struggles with an unfamiliar and scary criminal justice system and fights to regain control of her own future.

Chapter 10

DOMESTIC ABUSERS SHOULD BE ARRESTED

DOMESTIC ABUSERS SHOULD BE ARRESTED, PROSE-CUTED, AND JAILED FOR THE CRIMES THEY HAVE COMMITTED.

The statement above, a common sense approach toward domestic abuse cases, unfortunately, is frequently not followed by our criminal justice system. Domestic abusers are often *not* arrested, prosecuted, and jailed for their crimes against their mates. Until our society begins to take such cases seriously, we are unlikely to see much improvement in the satisfactory resolution of domestic disputes.

Mandatory Arrest Laws

One positive change in some jurisdictions has been the creation and implementation of laws which require police officers to arrest domestic batterers when certain statutorily-defined criteria are met. This author is convinced that such mandatory arrest laws are a positive step in the right direction in the fight against domestic abuse in our nation.

For an excellent compilation of the status of laws against domestic violence across our country, see "State Codes on Domestic Violence," by Barbara J. Hart, J.D., in *Juvenile and Family Court Journal,* 1992, Vol. 43, No. 4, available from Box 8970, Reno, Nevada 89507, (702) 784-6012.

Wisconsin, for example, has a mandatory arrest law governing certain limited types of domestic abuse situations. That law reads as follows:

968.075 Domestic abuse incidents; arrest and prosecution. (1) DEFINITIONS. In this section:

(a) "Domestic abuse" means any of the following engaged in by an adult person against his or her spouse or former spouse, against an adult with whom the person resides or formerly resided or against an adult with whom the person has created a child:

1. Intentional infliction of physical pain, physical injury or illness.

2. Intentional impairment of physical condition.

3. A violation of 940.225 (1), (2) or (3). (AUTHOR'S NOTE: THIS REFERS TO FIRST THROUGH FOURTH DEGREE SEXUAL ASSAULT AS DEFINED BY WISCONSIN STATUTES.)

4. A physical act that may cause the other person reasonably to fear imminent engagement in the conduct described under subd. 1, 2, or 3.

(b) "Law enforcement agency" has the meaning specified in s. 165.83(1)(b).

(2) CIRCUMSTANCES REQUIRING ARREST. (a) Notwithstanding s. 968.07 and except as provided in par. (b), a law enforcement officer shall arrest and take a person into custody if:

1. The officer has reasonable grounds to believe that the person is committing or has committed domestic abuse and that the person's actions constitute the commission of a crime; and

2. Either or both of the following circumstances are present:

a. The officer has a reasonable basis for believing that continued domestic abuse against the alleged victim is likely.

b. There is evidence of physical injury to the alleged victim.

(b) If the officer's reasonable grounds for belief under par. (a) 1 are based on a report of an alleged domestic abuse incident, the officer is required to make an arrest under par. (a) only if the report is received, within 28 days after the day the incident is alleged to have occurred, by the officer or the law enforcement agency that employs the officer.

(3) LAW ENFORCEMENT POLICIES. (a) Each law enforcement agency shall develop, adopt and implement written policies regarding arrest procedures for domestic abuse incidents. The policies shall include, but not be limited to, the following:

1. Statements emphasizing that:

a. In most circumstances, other than those under sub. (2), a law enforcement officer should arrest and take a person into custody if the officer has reasonable grounds to believe that the person is committing or had committed domestic abuse and that the person's actions constitute the commission of a crime.

b. When the officer has reasonable grounds to believe that spouses, former spouses or other persons who reside together or formerly resided together are committing or have committed domestic abuse against each other, the officer does not have to arrest both persons, but should arrest the person whom the officer believes to be the primary physical aggressor. In determining who is the primary physical aggressor, an officer should consider the intent of this section to protect victims of domestic violence, the relative degree of injury or fear inflicted on the persons involved and any history of domestic abuse between these persons, if that history can be reasonably ascertained by the officer.

c. A law enforcement officer's decision as to whether or not to arrest under this section may not be based on the consent of the victim to any subsequent prosecution or on the relationship of the persons involved in the incident.

d. A law enforcement officer's decision not to arrest under this section may not be based solely upon the absence of visible indications of injury or impairment.

2. A procedure for the written report and referral required under sub. (4).

3. A procedure for notifying the alleged victim of the incident of the provisions in sub. (5), the procedure for releasing the arrested person and the likelihood and probable time of the arrested person's release.

(b) In the development of these policies, each law enforcement agency is encouraged to consult with community organizations and other law enforcement agencies with expertise in the recognition and handling of domestic abuse incidents.

(c) This subsection does not limit the authority of a law enforcement agency to establish policies that require arrests under more circumstances than those set forth in sub. (2).

(4) REPORT REQUIRED WHERE NO ARREST. If a law enforcement officer does not make an arrest under this section when the officer has reasonable grounds to believe that a person is committing or has committed domestic abuse and that person's acts constitute the commission of a crime, the officer shall prepare a written report stating why the person was not arrested. The report shall be sent to the district attorney's office, in the county where the acts took place, immediately after investigation of the incident has been completed. The district attorney shall review the report to determine whether the person involved in the incident should be charged with the commission of a crime.

(5) CONTACT PROHIBITION. (a) 1. Unless there is a waiver under par. (c), during the 24 hours immediately following an arrest for a domestic abuse incident, the arrested person shall avoid the residence of the alleged victim of the domestic abuse incident and, if applicable, any premises temporarily occupied by the alleged victim, and avoid contacting or causing any person, other than law enforcement officers and attorneys for the arrested person and alleged victim, to contact the alleged victim.

2. An arrested person who intentionally violates this paragraph shall be required to forfeit not more than $1,000.

(b) 1. Unless there is a waiver under par. (c), a law enforcement officer or other person who releases a person arrested for a domestic abuse incident from custody less than 24 hours after the arrest shall inform the arrested person orally and in writing of the requirements under par. (a), the consequences of violating the requirements and the provisions of s. 939.621. The arrested person shall sign an acknowledgment on the written notice that he or she has received notice of, and understands the requirements, the consequences of violating the requirements and the provisions of s. 939.621. If the arrested person refuses to sign the notice, he or she may not be released from custody.

2. If there is a waiver under par. (c) and the person is released under subd. 1, the law enforcement officer or other person who releases the arrested person shall inform the arrested person orally and in writing of the waiver and the provisions of s. 939.621.

3. Failure to comply with the notice requirement under subd. 1 regarding a

person who is lawfully released from custody bars a prosecutions under par. (a), but does not affect the application of s. 939.621 in any criminal prosecution.

(c) At any time during the 24-hour period specified in par. (a), the alleged victim may sign a written waiver of the requirements of par. (a). The law enforcement agency shall have a waiver form available.

(d) The law enforcement agency responsible for the arrest of a person for a domestic abuse incident shall notify the alleged victim of the requirements under par. (a) and the possibility of, procedure for and effect of a waiver under par. (c).

(e) Notwithstanding s. 968.07, a law enforcement officer shall arrest and take a person into custody if the officer has reasonable grounds to believe that the person has violated par. (a).

(6) CONDITIONAL RELEASE. A person arrested and taken into custody for a domestic abuse incident is eligible for conditional release. Unless there is a waiver under sub. (5) (c), as part of the conditions of any such release that occurs during the 24 hours immediately following such an arrest, the person shall be required to comply with the requirements under sub. (5)(a) and to sign the acknowledgment under sub. (5)(b). The arrested person's release shall be conditioned upon his or her signed agreement to refrain from any threats or acts of domestic abuse against the alleged victim or other person.

(6m) OFFICER IMMUNITY. A law enforcement officer is immune from civil and criminal liability arising out of a decision by the officer to arrest or not arrest an alleged offender, if the decision is made in a good faith effort to comply with this section.

(7) PROSECUTION POLICIES. Each district attorney's office shall develop, adopt and implement written policies encouraging the prosecution of domestic abuse offenses. The policies shall include, but not be limited to, the following:

(a) A policy indicating that a prosecutor's decision not to prosecute a domestic abuse incident should not be based:

1. Solely upon the absence of visible indications of injury or impairment;

2. Upon the victim's consent to any subsequent prosecution of the other person involved in the incident; or

3. Upon the relationship of the persons involved in the incident.

(b) A policy indicating that when any domestic abuse incident is reported to the district attorney's office, including a report made under sub. (4), a charging decision by the district attorney should, absent extraordinary circumstances, be made not less than 2 weeks after the district attorney has received notice of the incident.

(8) EDUCATION AND TRAINING. Any education and training by the law enforcement agency relating to the handling of domestic abuse complaints shall stress enforcement of criminal laws in domestic abuse incidents and protection of the alleged victim. Law enforcement agencies and community organizations with expertise in the recognition and handling of domestic abuse incidents shall cooperate in all aspects of the training.

(9) ANNUAL REPORT. (a) Each district attorney shall submit an annual report to the department of justice listing all of the following:

1. The number of arrests for domestic abuse incidents in his or her county as compiled and furnished by the law enforcement agencies within the county.

2. The number of subsequent prosecutions and convictions of the persons arrested for domestic abuse incidents.

(b) The listing of the number of arrests, prosecutions and convictions under par. (a) shall include categories by statutory reference to the offense involved and include totals for all categories.

Defining Domestic Violence

This author believes that the definitions of domestic abuse in laws like that of Wisconsin need to be carefully looked at to make certain that the multitude of domestic living arrangements which exist in today's society are covered.

Among those persons whose domestic relationships should be covered are:

1. Spouses.

2. Persons who live together in the same household as girlfriend/boyfriend or lovers.

3. Persons who are intimately involved even if they do not live/reside in the same household.

4. Homosexual and lesbian relationships.

5. Persons who are dating each other but who have not been intimate.

6. Ex-spouses, ex-boyfriends, ex-girlfriends, and the like.

Domestic abuse, under Wisconsin law, includes sexual batteries/assaults/abuse—a common form of domestic abuse. The author would recommend that all states include sexual abuse in their domestic abuse laws.

Mandatory Prosecution

The failure to prosecute domestic abusers for the crimes of abuse they commit against their mates appears to be a major problem in certain jurisdictions. It is for this reason that this author recommends that state legislatures seriously consider passage of laws which would require prosecutors to charge and prosecute domestic abusers for their crimes, with very limited exceptions to those requirements, to be spelled out in the statutes.

Police Policies for Handling Domestic Abuse Incidents

Police departments throughout our nation, as a result of successful challenges by victims of domestic abuse to failures by police in some jurisdictions to protect them from their abusers, are tending to pay close attention to the handling of domestic abuse incidents, including by creation of departmental policies governing handling of such cases. The City of Milwaukee, Department of Police, for example, issued Order No. 10260 on May 8, 1990, which reads:

RE: CHANGES IN THE DOMESTIC ABUSE LAW, EFFECTIVE MAY 8, 1990

On Monday, April 23, 1990, Governor Tommy Thompson signed 1989 Wisconsin Act 293, commonly referred to as the Domestic Abuse Trailer Bill. This law revises certain portions of s. 968.075, the Domestic Abuse Law and becomes effective on tuesday, May 8, 1990. The changes in this law are subtle; however they will have a positive impact on our Department's domestic abuse policy. Limited discretion has been created and all domestic abuse offenses will no longer be considered mandatory arrest situations.

DOMESTIC ABUSE DEFINED

The definition of domestic abuse has been revised and is now defined as:

- intentional infliction of physical pain, physical injury, or illness;
- intentional impairment of physical condition;
- sexual assault (1st through 4th degree); or,
- a physical act that may cause the other person to reasonably fear imminent engagement in the conduct described above,

engaged in by an adult person against his or her spouse or former spouse, against an adult with whom the person resides or formerly resided, or against an adult with whom the person has created a child.

The list of adult relatives that was contained in the original law has been eliminated, although adult relatives are still covered under this revision if they reside together or formerly resided together. Also eliminated from the definition of domestic abuse is the term, "a threat in conjunction with a physical act." Threats alone no longer constitute a violation of the Domestic Abuse law and must be handled as non-domestic violence cases.

Complaints such as burglary, theft, entry into locked vehicle, and many criminal damage to property incidents will not qualify as domestic abuse cases. There must be evidence to indicate that these physical acts will reasonably lead the victim to fear imminent engagement in a battery or sexual assault. If this connection cannot be established, the incident must be handled as a non-domestic violence case.

MANDATORY ARREST REVISIONS

Under this revision, an officer shall arrest and take a person into custody if:

1) The officer has reasonable grounds to believe that the person is committing or has committed domestic abuse and that the person's actions constitute the commission of a crime. If the officer's reasonable grounds for belief are based on a report of an alleged domestic abuse incident, the officer is required to make an arrest only if the report is received within 28 days after the day the incident is alleged to have occurred, by the officer or law enforcement agency that employs the officer.

2) In addition to the above, either or both of the following circumstances must be present:
   a) the officer has a reasonable basis for believing that continued domestic abuse against the alleged victim is likely, and/or,
   b) there is evidence of physical injury to the alleged victim.

The law revision created two important changes in the mandatory arrest criteria. The first change revises the arrest criteria to focus on the likelihood of continued domestic abuse rather than the possibility of continued violence. The second revision recognizes a 28-day exception to the mandatory arrest policy. Under this second revision, if an officer is acting on the basis of a domestic abuse report that is received more than 28 days after the alleged incident occurred (excluding the date of the incident), the officer is not obligated to follow the arrest requirements of the law. In this situation, the officer follows arrest procedures applicable to crimes, generally, and an order-in would most likely occur.

With these revisions, a probable cause battery complaint involving pain but no injury, reported within 28 days of the date of the incident, requires a mandatory arrest only if the officer reasonably believes that continued domestic abuse is *likely*. The case would be handled as a non-arrest situation if the officer reasonably believes that continued domestic abuse is *unlikely* and would normally be ordered-in for review.

OFFICER DISCRETION

The revision of this law has created discretion for the officer in three separate areas. These situations are:

1) The officer may use discretion when determining whether any physical act by the suspect may cause the victim to reasonably fear imminent engagement in either a battery or sexual assault. If it is not reasonable to believe that a particular physical act by the suspect would result in either a battery or sexual assault to the victim, the incident would not qualify under the revised definition of domestic abuse and would be handled as a non-domestic violence case.

2) The officer can use discretion when investigating a probable cause domestic abuse incident where it is determined that the victim has suffered no physical injury and the officer reasonably believes that continued domes-

tic abuse against the victim is not likely. These situations can be handled as domestic violence order-in situations instead of making an arrest.

3) Discretion can always be used by the officer when determining the probable cause of any incident that is investigated.

24-HOUR NO CONTACT PERIOD

The original domestic abuse law prevented any contact with the victim during the 24-hour no-contact period which follows the defendant's arrest except for attorneys representing either the defendant or victim. The law revision authorizes law enforcement officers to contact the victim during this time period if the need arises.

IMMUNITY PROVISION FOR LAW ENFORCEMENT OFFICERS

The law revision created an immunity provision which protects a law enforcement officer from civil and criminal liability arising out of a decision by the officer to arrest or not arrest an alleged offender, providing the decision is made in a good faith effort to comply with the domestic abuse arrest statute.

The changes in the domestic abuse law will become effective on May 8, 1990.

Philip Arreola, Chief of Police

It is important to again emphasize that police departments need to have in place effective and understandable guidelines for the handling of domestic abuse situations. In the author's view, those guidelines should include the mandatory arrest of domestic abusers. It is also critical for police departments to train each and every department member in the handling of domestic abuse cases. Such training should utilize the team-teaching approach (police officer, prosecutor, domestic abuse center staff) and must be lengthy enough to be effective. In addition, updated training should be considered for in-service sessions from time to time, and law changes or changes in handling of such cases should be presented, as needed, at police roll calls.

Beware of Inaccurate Mandatory Arrest Study Results

In recent years, some studies have been conducted concerning the impact of mandatory arrest by police on domestic abuse situations. Some of these studies suggest that such arrests have little or no positive impact and may, in fact, result in worse abuse of persons, in some cases.

This author takes issue with those studies which are, in her view, inaccurate. It is simply illogical to suggest or conclude that holding abusers accountable (by arrest) would not tend to help the abused persons overcome and end the abuse. Common sense tells us that once the abuse is out in the open and made public by arrest and prosecution, that it is less likely to occur again, especially assuming that many of the abuse victims will have also received help in ending the abuse through restraining orders, counseling, ending the relationship, and other means.

Study results which suggest that mandatory arrest has not been effective are based upon a selection of the wrong types of cases to study. Namely, the studies were done in places where mandatory arrest was not (except in a few cases) followed up by the necessary second step to make such arrests effective—the prosecution of the abusers. Common sense dictates that arrest without prosecution would have little long-term deterrent impact. This author cautions readers against granting credibility to studies done concerning mandatory arrest cases where prosecution of the batterers did not take place.

We must be concerned about attempts by persons to use illogical study results to try to do away with mandatory arrest of domestic abusers laws. Mandatory arrest is needed because some police officers still retain a false view that domestic abuse is a "family matter" and do not take such cases seriously or want to treat such behavior as a crime. Our society cannot afford to leave it to the discretion of such police officers to arrest or not arrest domestic abusers. The vast majority of police officers are presumably sensitive to the reality of the dynamics of domestic abuse situations and are inclined to treat such incidents as serious matters.

CONCLUSION

The police play a major role in the fight against domestic abuse in our communities. They are often the first professionals to be made aware that abuse has taken place between specific mates. Therefore, they are in the unique position of being able to make a positive impression on the victim of the crime of domestic abuse—by arresting the abuser and helping the victim to obtain help from other resources (shelter; restraining orders; counseling; financial aid; child care; medical care, etc.). The failure of a police officer to treat a domestic abuse case seriously can give a victim the impression that the criminal justice system will not help her to end the abuse or hold her abuser accountable—with the result that she or he may continue to tolerate such abuse.

The author firmly believes that police, working in a positive networking relationship with other providers of help to victims of abuse, can successfully prevent domestic abuse in the lives of abuse victims.

Chapter 11

DOMESTIC ABUSERS SHOULD BE PROSECUTED

A major way in which our criminal justice system fails battered women is when prosecutors make negligent and willful decisions not to charge and prosecute domestic abusers with the crime of battery (or other appropriate charges like attempted homicide, or violations of domestic abuse restraining orders, or weapons offenses). Throughout our nation such cases are not being taken seriously by some of the district attorneys/states attorneys whom the public elects to prosecute persons who have committed crimes. This failure is a major roadblock to the efforts of abuse-fighting professionals to reduce domestic violence in our society.

The impact this failure has on the attitudes and behavior of batterers was discussed in Chapter 5. This chapter focuses on the need to hold batterers accountable for their conduct by prosecuting them as the criminals they truly are.

101 Lame and Not so Lame Excuses to Let Domestic Batterers Cop Pleas to Lesser Charges

Some of the players in the criminal justice game remind me of the puppies in the Walt Disney movie "101 Dalmations." They are like a bunch of spotted puppy dogs running around wildly, as uncertain of how to behave as puppies are. Except that the "spots" in the criminal justice system are symptoms of decay, whereas the spots on dalmations are part of the way God created them.

There is no question that prosecutors must have *some* discretion in handling domestic violence battery cases. I firmly believe that discretion must be limited by effective and properly written prosecutorial office guidelines *or* passage of a law by the legislatures which mandates that such cases be prosecuted as batteries—absent substantial justification in an individual case to treat it differently. The guidelines or the statute would have to list reasons which would be sufficient cause to reduce or dismiss domestic battery charges, while also allowing for additional reasons which could be shown to be reasonable and justifiable. The law or guidelines would, importantly, make it clear that public policy interests dictate that persons arrested for domestic battery be prosecuted as batterers absent good cause shown in individual cases.

The following list of possible reasons for reducing or dropping domestic battery charges is offered. Some of these are justifiable, and some are clearly not.

1. That's how the criminal justice system works.

2. The batterer in the case faces first degree murder charges for killing the woman he abused.

3. The battered woman killed the batterer in self-defense and he is not going to batter her or anyone else ever again.

4. The ADA in charge of the case is sympathetic to the batterer because he is a domestic abuser himself.

5. Insufficient evidence to prove guilt beyond a reasonable doubt exists.

6. The DA only wants those cases which are clearly going to be won at trial prosecuted.

7. Taking cases to trial will take up too much court time.

8. The DA's office doesn't have enough staff to investigate and try these cases.

9. There isn't enough space in the jail for thousands of domestic batterers each year.

10. The victim of the battery refuses to cooperate and there isn't sufficient evidence to convict the batterer without her cooperation and testimony.

11. The batterer is being defended by a well-known defense attorney with a record of winning cases.

12. The batterer is well-known in the community.

13. The police "misplaced" evidence critical to winning the case.

14. Someone got paid off.

15. The judge the case is pending before has a history of refusing to sentence convicted domestic batterers to jail time.

16. Prosecution should be deferred because the batterer has agreed to enter a batterer's program.

17. The victim's story is not credible because it is contradicted by physical evidence or believable eyewitness accounts.

18. There are credible reasons to believe the victim will be in more danger if the batterer is prosecuted than if he is not.

19. The batterer has a provable alibi showing he was elsewhere at the time of the alleged crime.

20. The statute of limitations for prosecuting the battery has run out.

21. The victim pleads with the DA's office not to prosecute.

22. The victim recants her claim that the batterer battered her and now claims he did not do so.

23. The defense plans to present expert testimony which would successfully contradict the victim's story.

24. The case won't go to trial for over a year.

25. Medical testimony by the defense would effectively call the victim's version of what happened into question.

26. Cases reduced to civil ordinance violations are easier to win because of a lower burden of proof.

27. The victim has a history of criminal behavior or of mental health problems which could reduce her credibility.

28. The batterer passes a lie detector test indicating he didn't commit the battery.

29. The victim loves the abuser and doesn't want him prosecuted.

30. The injury sustained by the victim was minor.

A well-thought-out list prepared by a task force of professionals who deal with domestic violence cases and problems would be helpful to prosecutors or the state legislature in acting upon this important issue. The clearly unjustifiable reasons for not prosecuting domestic batterers listed above are numbers 1, 4, 11, 12, 14, 15, 26, and 28.

A variety of the other reasons given are also unjustifiable because they are based on the failure of our society to properly fund necessary criminal justice services like jails, prosecutors, police, courts, etc. They are not based on legitimate issues involving the merits of particular domestic abuse cases. These unjustifiable, criminal justice system related reasons are: 7, 8, 9, and 24.

The other excuses raised in the hypothetical set of reasons merit individual discussion.

2. A prosecutor faced with a murder case against a batterer might legitimately dismiss battery charges as unnecessary.

3. If the batterer is dead, he obviously can't be prosecuted for battery. However, the woman who killed her abuser in self-defense should not be

prosecuted for murder or any other crime. Her actions were justifiable, and she committed no crime.

5-6. There will always be credibility issues in domestic abuse cases (see Chapter 7). Most cases will, inevitably, involve the woman victim's word against that of her male batterer. It is time we recognized that the woman's word, *alone* (even absent provable physical injury), will constitute guilt beyond a reasonable doubt.

It is never legitimate for a district attorney to prosecute only those cases which are clearly going to be won at trial. Such an attitude would result in most domestic abuse cases not being prosecuted because it is next to impossible to predict whether these cases will be won if they wind up going to trial as batteries. District attorneys who are concerned about how successful or unsuccessful they will appear to their public, the press, and their political supporters regarding winning and losing cases should realize that they will have built up a disgraceful record of losses whenever they fail to properly prosecute domestic abusers for battery or other appropriate charges. This is true because these criminals will have escaped just prosecution and punishment for these crimes. In addition, such prosecutors will have virtually guaranteed the future abuse of the abused women. This is expediency, not justice.

10 and 21. Prosecutors must not listen to pleas from victims of domestic abuse not to prosecute. The refusal of the victim to cooperate is something prosecutors will face in at least one-half of the domestic abuse cases they handle. The reasons for this can be found in the sociological and psychological attitudes and behavior patterns of abused women, most particularly their learned helplessness and their fear of retaliation by their batterers. Prosecutors must not use this as an excuse to drop or fail to bring domestic abuse cases. If the victim told a cop or someone else that the batterer battered her, the prosecutor should use that person's testimony. Subpoena the victim to testify. Use other evidence that abuse occurred—if it exists (such as photographs, medical data, witnesses, etc.). If the victim lies under oath, it is possible that the judge or jury will recognize, from her demeanor, and other facts of the case, that she is lying by claiming she was not abused. Impeach her with prior statements, and other people's testimony, where available. Use experts to identify, for the judge or jury, why a battered woman might lie about her abuse. Prosecutors who drop charges against batterers when victims of domestic abuse are uncooperative, hostile, or unreliable, are doing these victims a huge disfavor. Her refusing to cooperate could give an abuser the ability

to, without opposition from the criminal justice system, batter her again. The failure of a victim of the crime of domestic battery to support the prosecutor's efforts to hold her abuser accountable is not a valid reason to drop a case. Victims must be told that the state, not they, are bringing criminal charges against the batterers, and that the prosecutors' charges will not be dropped.

13. Misplacement, by police, of critical evidence may make a domestic abuse case harder to win. However, most such cases rely primarily on testimony of victims and abusers, not on physical evidence. The physical evidence is often a backup to the victim's claims of abuse. Such cases should be prosecuted, despite the missing physical evidence, if at all possible.

16. It is legitimate, in *some* cases, to defer prosecution when a batterer has agreed to enter a batterers' program. Prosecutors should make certain the batterers in question actually *complete* the program successfully. Batterers have a tendency to try to play games with the system, and one of the games is to promise to get counseling, and to promise to complete a batterers' program, with no real intention of doing this. Any new incidents of abuse should be vigorously prosecuted. The system needs to realize that, in order to deal effectively with domestic violence as a societal problem, it must make many more batterers' programs available.

17. In cases in which a victim's story is not credible, efforts must be made to get the full truth from the victim. It may be that she has lied about some aspect of the situation, as a result of her suffering from the Battered Woman syndrome. It could be that she is telling the truth and her story merely sounds bizarre. Or it could be that an eyewitness whose account contradicts that of the victim is lying. In such cases more investigation needs to be done.

18. It is only in extremely rare cases where a victim is in more danger if a batterer is prosecuted than if he is not. The problem is that most victims believe that they are putting themselves in a great deal more danger (from retribution by the batterer) if they cooperate in turning the abuser in to authorities and in his prosecution for battery. This is a legitimate fear. However, doing nothing, and not cooperating, also does not solve the problem. While a batterer *may* retaliate (if he is not kept away from the victim with a restraining order which is enforced, if necessary), he also may not. Some batterers get scared out of their abusive behavior, at least temporarily, by the fact that the system (police, prosecutors, social workers, etc.) is on to them (i.e., that his abuse of his

mate has been exposed to the light of day instead of continuing to be a hidden crime). There is no doubt, however, that if a batterer is *not* prosecuted, the future escalating and more frequent abuse of the victim is virtually guaranteed.

19. If the batterer's alibi is a good one, the victim is lying. Find out, if that is the case, *why* she would make up such a story. Victims usually don't. Perhaps the explanation is something as simple as someone, probably the victim, getting the date when the battery occurred, wrong.

20. *Statutes of limitations for domestic batteries should be eliminated by legislatures.* The lives battered and abused women live are similar to the lives of other abuse victims such as victims of incest or child molesting or sexual misconduct by therapists. Battered women often do not recognize themselves as victims of abuse while the abuse is going on, or they block the truth from their minds so effectively, or live in such fear of doing something about the abuse, that statutes of limitation regarding some of the more severe incidents of abuse may have passed by the time the victim tries to do something about the abuse. Therefore, if it can be shown that the abuser pushed a victim down a flight of stairs ten years earlier, causing her leg to be broken, that should be a prosecutable offense when the victim finally comes forward with the truth and seeks help from the system, to cite just one example.

23. "Expert" testimony is something which persons working within the criminal justice system and "experts" recognize as a commodity which is bought and sold to the highest bidder. There are a lot of good and a lot of bad "experts" out there who will testify in court for the right price, or, in some cases, out of genuine dedication to their field of expertise/work. When the defense in a domestic battery case offers an expert to testify, prosecutors should counter this by using their own experts and/or challenging the qualifications, bias, or findings of the defense expert.

25. When issues of medical testimony by experts arise, the prosecution must consider how legitimate and damaging the testimony may be. Can it be countered by a prosecution medical expert? Remember that it is common for domestic abuse victims to lie to doctors and nurses about how their injuries occurred. Therefore, if her doctor's notes say that she got a black eye by bumping into a door, for example, this could be countered by having her testify that she lied to the doctor, and telling why, and perhaps even by asking the doctor whether he or she believed

that's how she got the injury and whether the injury was consistent with bumping into a door and/or being hit in the eye by a fist.

27. A victim's history of mental or physical health problems, if made an issue in a case or trial, need not necessarily destroy her credibility. The fact is that such problems, in abuse cases, may well be the result of the victim's domestic abuse and/or childhood physical, sexual, or emotional abuse—and need not harm the prosecutor's case when shown to be due to this.

Some domestic violence victims will have histories of "criminal" behavior. The crimes are usually ones like shoplifting, or welfare fraud, or petty theft. In other words, these criminal acts can be shown to have resulted from her desperation to economically/financially care for her family. While such criminal acts are not excusable or justifiable, they may well be explainable in a manner which will not seriously damage her credibility. It is also well known within the abuse-fighting profession that female victims of domestic abuse are often forced by their abusers to commit the sorts of crimes just described, or other crimes like drug dealing. These female victims of abuse, in those cases, might well have cooperated with the abusers' demands out of fear. This sort of history should not jeopardize a domestic abuse case if it is explained by a caring, effective prosecutor. It may be possible to keep such evidence out of the record entirely as not relevant to her claims of domestic abuse, just as prior bad acts and prior crime evidence is frequently kept out of evidence in cases as highly prejudicial to criminal defendants.

29. The victim's love for her abuser will often arise as a reason for her pleading with a prosecutor not to jail, or prosecute her abuser. Prosecutors must remember that most of the victims of domestic abuse they will encounter are still in love with their abusers, blame themselves for their victimization, are not necessarily ready to end the violent relationship, think he will change, and have bought into the lies the abuser has told them in the past in order to ensure continuation of the relationship. That is why it is so critical that, by the time the victim deals seriously with the prosecutor about her case, she has already been counseled by the staff of a local domestic abuse center, been helped to obtain a restraining order, if needed, and been offered other options to continuing abuse. The "love" issue is a very delicate one which prosecutors must be prepared to handle in most of these cases. The victim still loves the abuser and believes that he loves her (see Chapter 4). If abuse in a relationship is not stopped, the love a victim has for her abuser eventually dies. But it

takes time for this to happen. Prosecutors must not let victims' claims that they "love" the abuser and believe that things will truly get better prevent them from prosecuting batterers for their crimes.

30. Laws which govern assaults and/or batteries, by definition, do not always require that a physical injury result from the assault or battery in order for a crime to have been committed. For example, slapping someone, with no resultant bruise or physical injury, may still qualify as a violation of the law. Prosecutors faced with domestic abuse situations where an assault such as slapping, or rape has taken place need to carefully look at the legal options in what specific crimes may be determined to have occurred in such situations—and charge the abusers accordingly, with the toughest possible offenses. The lack of physical evidence of a battery or an assault is not a reason to decline to prosecute domestic abuse cases.

In sum, there are many more valid and invalid reasons which prosecutors might consider in making charging and other prosecutorial decisions in domestic abuse cases. This author has listed only a handful of these (rather than attempting to create 101) to encourage professionals to look seriously at this important aspect of domestic abuse cases. The point to be emphasized is that widespread discretion in the hands of prosecutors and assistant prosecutors is unwise in these cases. Legislatures in states where prosecutors can be shown to not be taking domestic abuse cases seriously should consider passing laws to mandate prosecution of such cases (with reasonable exceptions to permit for reasonable discretion in such cases, possibly by letting judges decide if prosecutorial decisions not to prosecute, on an individual case basis, are justified). In addition, prosecutors should be guiding the discretion and decision-making of their staff in the handling of domestic abuse cases so that certain procedures are followed in charging, prosecuting, and, plea bargaining of such cases. Strong and effective prosecutorial guidelines, issued from the prosecutor, are needed in this area of the law.

No Lesser Plea!

This part of this chapter is written to prosecutors.

Dropping domestic battery cases, or reducing them to lesser charges, or to inappropriate disorderly conduct civil ordinance violations makes a mockery of justice and revictimizes the victims.

Surely *you* do not condone this.

Is this "justice"?

I do not believe it is justice.

Not under my concept of justice—a search for the truth followed by a fair outcome of a case. I do not believe your concept of justice differs from mine.

Why, then, do the statistics demonstrate such an appalling record of failure in domestic violence cases which are handled by your office?

There should be no lesser acceptable plea in most domestic abuse cases. These are batteries and should be treated as such. Absent sufficient justification to treat them differently.

Your prosecutorial guidelines for handling domestic abuse cases should be drafted in a way as to make that stance clear.

If you agree with me that that is the proper way to handle such cases.

You would no doubt remind me that the criminal justice system discourages jail time because of overcrowded jails, and encourages plea bargains and dismissals in order to reduce court costs and staffing costs. And that civil ordinance disorderly conduct cases carry a lesser burden of proof than proof beyond a reasonable doubt.

My answer to you would be, "The system be damned!"

The "system" as we know it is not functioning.

We all know it.

Do we fear to act to change it?

Or consider this an impossible task?

Why not tell it like it is.

And force the politicians to seriously address these issues.

If that kind of attitude is idealistic, so be it.

Throughout history, positive change has been brought about by those people who dared to be different, who challenged the status quo, who dared to dream and to make their dreams reality.

That is my attitude. I suspect you are somewhat of an idealist too, with your idealism scarred by the unpleasant reality you face every day in the criminal justice system.

I am suggesting that that reality—a system mired in the ugly mud of criminal behavior and social injustice—must change.

For the good, health, welfare, safety, and prosperity of all.

To tolerate such a system is intolerable.

To call this a system of "justice" is itself unjust.

To hammer away, day by day by day, making tiny, ineffective dents in this massive problem is stupidity at its finest.

Why not strive for excellence in criminal justice instead?

Joseph Pulitzer wrote in the *St. Louis Post Dispatch* on April 10, 1907:

> I know that my retirement will make no difference in its cardinal principles, that it will always fight for progress and reform, never tolerate injustice or corruption, always fight demagogues of all parties, never belong to any party, always oppose privileged classes and public plunderers, never lack sympathy with the poor, always remain devoted to the public welfare, never be satisfied with merely printing news, never be afraid to attack wrong, whether by predatory plutocracy or predatory poverty.

The values cited by Mr. Pulitzer are sound ones, rooted in concepts of social justice and morality and goodness.

We must not hesitate to attack the wrong of domestic violence.

To attack domestic abuse *is* fighting for progress and reform. It is a demonstration of devotion to the public welfare and of service to humanity. Domestic violence is, in itself, a form of injustice—unjust treatment of people—and it is a form of corruption of human morality.

John F. Kennedy wrote about the concept of human morality in *Profiles In Courage:*

> The same basic choice of courage or compliance continually faces us all. . . . A man does what he must—in spite of obstacles and dangers and pressures—and that is the basis of all human morality.

In my viewpoint, John Kennedy was trying to say that we have to find the courage *to do what is right*—even when it means losing income, friends, employment, support, political power, and happiness. When we do something wrong it burdens our conscience, as it rightly should.

For me, it feels right to mount the strongest possible attack on domestic violence in our community, no matter what consequences such a position has for my professional and personal life.

We need to devote substantially more governmental and societal time and finances to attacking the domestic violence evil.

Perhaps I write too much philosophy about this issue. Yet, without a solid position grounded in philosophical principles, concrete solutions cannot be sought and found and implemented.

If you were ever to accuse me of being too much of an idealist and a dreamer, I would plead guilty. I see beyond the obvious facts in cases and search for uncommon solutions.

You must have had this kind of idealism and goals for reforming the system when you took on the task of becoming D.A. I believe you still have some of this idealism. We must never be afraid to act on that idealism or pursue our goals. That sort of thinking is in some people's souls. Idealists are the people who find the courage and the compassion to tackle and solve the problems in our society. Everyone else is part of the problem, sitting back contributing nothing positive, or busily telling us why something can't be done, and that we'd be fools for imagining it could be done and even greater fools for trying to do it. I say the most foolish thing of all would be to fail to try to make our world better.

The idealist in me knows we *can* reduce domestic violence in our nation.

If we make the effort to do so.

If we do not make that effort we are like a ship of fools about to sink into the depths of depravity, immorality, injustice, and hopeless indifference.

This is not an issue I can be indifferent to.

Nor is it an issue you can be indifferent to.

We have too much to lose, as a community, if we fail to attempt to resolve domestic violence problems.

It is not enough for us to proclaim our opposition to domestic violence. If we do not back our words with the actions and the resources necessary to make a real impact on this problem we are engaging in the sort of misleading rhetoric demogogic politicians use and resolving nothing.

We must be open-minded enough to recognize that the resolutions to domestic abuse problems may not lie in the same approaches used to date. These approaches may need to be complemented by new and as yet undiscovered innovative approaches. We must search for those solutions until they are found.

By now you are probably thinking what a lot of philosophical nonsense and hogwash some of this is.

From the standpoint of an experienced prosecutor whose decisions are grounded in pragmatism and logic.

There's nothing logical about domestic violence. In the volatile, unpredictable arena of domestic abuse, pragmatism alone will not solve the problem. It is our moral responsibility to move beyond pragmatism and logic and to consider concepts of faith and philosophy as we seek genuine solutions to this tragic problem. I don't think that's too much to hope for. Philosophers, and dreamers, and idealists are the people who accomplish great things in the world. They don't sit back and do what everybody else is doing. They creatively do different things. They strive to make good things better and to eliminate bad things from our society.

As President John F. Kennedy said in 1963:

I look forward to a great future for America, a future in which our country will match its military strength with our moral strength, its wealth with our wisdom, its power with our purpose. I look forward to an America which will not be afraid of grace and beauty, which will protect the beauty of our natural environment, which will preserve the great old American houses and squares and parks of our national past, and which will build handsome and balanced cities for our future. . . . And I look forward to an America which commands respect throughout the world not only for its strength but for its civilization as well.

If we, as individuals, and as a society, have the resources and the ability to mount a fierce attack on domestic violence, are we not failing to use our God-given talents if we neglect to fight the battle against this great evil which exists in our nation?

We have a *duty* to protect persons who cannot protect themselves, to help persons who cannot help themselves, to do good works and fight evil, and to do everything in our power to make our world better. I have no doubt that you share this sense of duty to humanity.

Won't you please listen to this passionate plea for you to change the way your office handles domestic disputes?

Chapter 12

THE PROSECUTOR'S ROLE

The role played by prosecutors in combating domestic violence is absolutely critical.

Prosecution of domestic abusers is an important part of ending domestic violence in individual relationships. The failure to prosecute encourages abusers to continue their criminal acts of violence toward their victims.

Victims of the crime of domestic violence need *someone* to trust, to believe in them, to rely on, to be there for them, and to help them end the pattern of abuse in their lives. Prosecutors, who are in a position of power to hold domestic abusers accountable for their illegal and wrongful acts of violence against their mates, can fill that critical role for these victims. Prosecutors, working together skillfully with other players in the fight against domestic abuse (police; social workers; domestic abuse shelter staff; doctors/nurses; financial aid representatives; judges; educators, etc.) are an important link in the process of resolving individual cases of domestic abuse and of taking steps to change abusive behavior of batterers.

Other parts of this book deal with a variety of aspects of the prosecution of domestic abusers. This chapter addresses prosecutorial options in handling domestic abuse cases.

Prosecutorial Options in Handling Domestic Abuse Cases

The fact that domestic abuse batteries, sexual assaults, or other crimes are committed by men or women against their mates does not make these wrongful acts any less important, any less criminal, or any less worthy of serious treatment and prosecution by our legal system that similar acts committed against strangers. This is the reality that prosecutors must keep in mind when faced with a multitude of domestic abuse cases each year in their communities. Prosecutors must, in their hearts, believe that domestic violence is as serious, if not more so, than other similar criminal acts (such as battery or sexual assault) involving strangers. And they must take action to treat such crimes with appropriate seriousness. In many cases the result of a serious consideration of domestic abuse cases will be to prosecute domestic abusers as the criminals they are—instead of dismissing charges or having civil charges brought. Fairness dictates no lesser result.

1. Preventing Future Violence

Prosecutors have an important role to play in preventing future domestic abuse incidents in individual relationships. They have access to the data (history of abuse, assuming the right questions are asked of abuse victims) and the victims which will enable them to isolate and give special attention to those cases which are most likely to result in highly dangerous future injury to persons or death. Prosecutors have access to police reports, witness statements, criminal histories of perpetrators, and other information which can give them the ability to spot the most dangerous cases and to handle such cases accordingly. In addition, prosecutors, in this author's view, have a public obligation to do everything within their power, to take action to stop the violence in the domestic abuse relationships which they are made aware of. This includes not only prosecution of offenders, and fighting for appropriate jail terms for offenders and/or deferred prosecution into batterers' programs aimed at changing abusive behavior, but it also includes making certain that individual victims receive the help they need in the form of support services, options and other counseling, safe places to go, obtaining restraining orders, enforcement of restraining orders, financial aid, child care services, education/job training, medical care, etc. In short, prosecutors have a duty to take these cases seriously and to treat them as such.

The unique access prosecutors have to the victims of the domestic abuse crimes and to their abuse histories can enable them to pinpoint cases in which the potential for future deadly or serious violence is likely. In this author's view, the signs of potential deadly or serious violence in domestic abuse relationships include the following:

a. If the female abuse victim starts dreaming, daydreaming, thinking, or talking, even in jest, about killing the abuser and thinks of or gives specifics of how to carry out such a killing. (The author notes that many battered women who kill their abuser have experienced these sorts of thoughts for some time prior to the occasion on which they acted to end their abuse by killing their mate.) Anyone, professional or friend, who hears an abuse victim speak of killing her mate must take such thoughts seriously and work very hard to get her the help she needs to end the relationship or to change the batterer's conduct into nonabusive behavior.

b. If the severity of the violence becomes extreme. Any serious injuries should be seen as a potential forerunner of even more deadly violence by professionals who treat such injuries, persons who work with victims of domestic abuse, and lay persons who notice such injuries in their friends. Obviously there will be disagreements over what is serious violence. However, things like broken bones, severe sexual assaults/injuries, signs of choking, severe beatings/bruises, gunshot or knife wounds, happening to either abuse victim or abuser, are cause to be concerned about the potential for even more deadly violence in the relationship. It is important to note that all domestic abuse cases deserve serious attention from our criminal justice system, aimed at preventing future abuse. However, certain cases deserve attention beyond the ordinary caring response domestic abuse victims deserve to receive from the system. The failure to take action to end the abuse in some cases can be fatal to victim and/or abuser.

c. A third factor indicative of the potential for future serious or fatal domestic violence is the escalation of the frequency of the violence in an intimate relationship. Clearly, *any* abuse in an intimate relationship is cause for concern on the part of the victim and society. Cases where there is reason to believe that the frequency of the abuse is escalating noticeably give cause for special concern. In other words, prosecutors and other professionals who handle such cases should isolate such cases and give them extra attention. Homes where police are frequently called to handle domestic disputes, families where victims frequently call domestic abuse centers for counseling or other help, and situations where the frequency of abusive incidents is increasing noticeably must be looked at seriously by the system. Of course, many cases involving domestic abuse have, as part of their history, a long-standing history of abuse which has gone unreported to authorities. It is, therefore, especially important for prosecutors to obtain detailed histories of abuse from all victims with whom they have contact. It seems that the more frequent the abuse, the more likely that such abuse will become more violent and more dangerous. Cases where there is a pattern of frequent or increasingly frequent abuse need to be examined closely by prosecutors or other authorities within the system who are assigned to that specific task.

d. If the abuser makes a sudden threat to the victim's children, or abuses the children, the likelihood that the female victim of domestic violence will strike back against the abuser with deadly force and cause severe injury or death becomes more likely. Although many domestic abuse victims will tolerate a great deal of domestic abuse toward themselves, when their children are physically harmed or threatened, they are more likely to act to stop the abusive behavior of the batterer. Sometimes this reaction takes the form of the victim seeking help from the resources available to stop domestic abuse. Sometimes it causes her to strike back against the abuser with deadly force—in self-defense to protect her children.

e. It is common, in abusive relationships, for the abusive partner to be jealous of the mate he or she victimizes. This jealousy takes the form of wild accusations about infidelity, and isolating the victim from her family, friends, and coworkers. In some cases it is clear that the jealousy of the abuser is so extreme as to present a severe danger to the victim. In other words, the excessive jealousy, and unfounded paranoia on the part of the abuser, such as the belief that the victim is involved in infidelity and/or an unwillingness to allow her to spend time with her family, friends, or persons other than the abuser, is so great, or extreme, that it could cause the abuser to injure the victim severely or even kill her. Obviously, it takes a lot of judgment on the part of persons working to end domestic abuse to determine which cases that come across their desks present this kind of potential threat to abuse victims. However, if the abuser is constantly spying on the victim, has her totally isolated, constantly accuses her of infidelity, won't let her work, won't let her be with friends or family, and acts pathologically jealous, there is more cause for concern than in cases where this is not taking place. These cases also present more difficulty when the victim decides to end the abusive relationship, for some of these jealous abusive men will attempt to follow the victim wherever she goes and to prevent her from becoming intimately involved with other men. Signs of pathological jealousy on the part of the abuser must be cause for concern for prosecutors and others who are trying to help the victim end the abuse. The need to protect such victims is greater, as is the need to attempt to change the batterers' attitudes and behavior.

Sometimes the separation of the parties—by restraining order, sheltering of the victim, divorce proceedings being started, etc. causes the abuser to become more dangerous and threatening to the victim than he was before. We must take care, as professionals, and persons who are concerned about the safety of domestic abuse victims, to take note if an abuser keeps trying to get back together with his former mate in an obsessive or particularly noticeable or dangerous way. Such behavior, if excessive, could pose a very serious threat to the future safety of the abuse victim, because it could result in deadly or serious violence toward her.

2. Criminal Charges

The strongest option available to prosecutors in handling domestic abuse cases is to issue criminal charges (which carry with them the potential for jail or prison time) against domestic abusers. It is the belief of this author that such charges are usually appropriate whenever acts of physical violence or sexual abuse against a mate have occurred.

Among the criminal charges which may apply to the nature of the acts committed by the abuser against his or her mate are these:

a. Battery. (This can vary in degree and the nature of the appropriate charge and penalty, based on the nature of the injury inflicted upon the domestic abuse victim).

b. Sexual assault. Sexual assaults committed by abusers upon their mates should be prosecuted as the crimes they are. Any unwanted sexual contact, even between a husband and a wife, is an assault.

c. Attempted murder. In severe cases, a charge of attempted murder may be an appropriate one.

d. Criminal disorderly conduct.

e. Criminal charges for violations by abusers of domestic abuse restraining orders. This is an important part of the enforcement mechanism concerning restraining orders. It is critical that prosecutors take such violations seriously and issue charges against abusers who violate the terms of such no-contact orders.

3. Charging Conferences

Some prosecutors' offices have developed systems under which domestic abuse victims have meetings with prosecutors to discuss the facts of their individual abuse histories and to determine what criminal charges, if any, should be brought against the domestic abusers. This author firmly objects to the use of such conferences to decide not to bring charges, and to prosecutors using their discretion in a way in which domestic abuse victims' pleas that their abusers not be prosecuted are listened to with the result that charges are not brought. Victims need to be firmly told that a crime has been committed and that the prosecutor intends to hold the abusers accountable for their acts of abuse. A properly run charging conference can be helpful in determining appropriate charges, determining the nature and dangerousness of the abuse which occurred, ensuring victim cooperation in the prosecution, and making referrals for where victims should seek help to end their abusive relationships. In some cases such conferences may result in a decision that deferred prosecution would be appropriate.

4. Deferred Prosecution

Deferred prosecution, in which the parties agree that the abuser will not be prosecuted unless he or she fails to successfully complete a batterers' program (aimed at ending his or her abusive behavior patterns), is appropriate in some cases. Prosecutors must exercise care in selecting which cases are appropriate for deferred prosecution. It is important that the entire criminal justice system recognize the value of batterers' programs, and provide enough such programs, and enough spots for batterers in such programs to make this option available to widespread numbers of abusers. Positive results have been reported by some of these programs. We, as a society, have to be willing to take a chance, at least in some abusive relationships, that the abusive behavior and attitudes of the abuser could be ended and the relationship could continue in a nonabusive manner. Obviously such an outcome will not be possible in some types of abusive situations. However, when this option is appropriate, it should be considered and used. Persons who fail to complete batterers' programs or who abuse their mate after having completed such programs should be prosecuted for their criminal acts of abuse. In addition, some incidents of domestic abuse are so severe, or the history of abuse is so severe, that criminal charges should be persued regardless of whether an abuser might be helped by or agree to participate in a batterers' program.

5. Referrals

Prosecutors should either provide appropriate services to victims of domestic abuse as part of their victim/witness programs, or make appropriate referrals to agencies which provide such services. Prosecutors should make certain that the victims who are seen by their office receive the following sorts of help:

   a. Counseling
   b. Safety (Shelters)

   c. Restraining orders
   d. Child care
   e. Financial aid
   f. Education or job training where needed
   g. Contact with other appropriate social service agencies
   h. Support services in helping the victims adapt to the nature of the criminal prosecution and civil court processes, including support in court testimony
   i. Legal help to obtain separations, divorces, child support, alimony, etc.
   j. Support, if possible, from family members or friends

6. Dropping Charges

Prosecutors should prosecute domestic abusers for the crimes they have committed unless reasonable grounds exist to decline to prosecute or to drop charges. In most cases, the only reasonable grounds which could exist to drop a prosecution of a domestic abuser is if the prosecutor were to become convinced that the abuse alleged, or the abuse for which the abuser was arrested, did not occur. Prosecutors must exercise care not to be fooled by the statements of victims of domestic violence retracting allegations of abuse. It is part of the nature of suffering from domestic abuse for such victims to deny that the abuse took place. Pleas of victims to drop charges, and a refusal to cooperate in prosecution of abusive mates, are not, usually, grounds for a prosecutor to drop charges of battery, sexual assault, or other domestic abuse crimes. It must be made clear to victims and abusers that the state, the police/prosecutor, *not* the victim of the domestic abuse, is bringing criminal charges against the abuser. Victims must not be made to sign criminal complaints against their abusers. Such complaints should be signed by police officers, in the same way criminal complaints are signed by such officers in other types of criminal prosecutions. It is the state, not the abuse victim, who is holding the abuser accountable for his acts of abuse.

7. Criminal versus Civil Charges

Some localities follow a practice of refusing to charge domestic abusers with the crime of battery. These prosecutors often refer domestic abuse cases to city attorneys for consideration of bringing noncriminal municipal ordinance charges such as disorderly conduct. Such civil charges carry only a fine as a penalty, do not need to be proven beyond a reasonable doubt (like criminal cases do), and carry no potential jail or prison time. In addition, batterers who have their acts of abuse treated as civil ordinance violations do not get any sort of a criminal record as a result of their offenses. This author strongly believes that it is usually an inappropriate option for a county prosecutor to transfer a domestic abuse case to a city attorney's office for charging as a civil offense. Most of these domestic abuse cases involve crimes. The appropriate charge for commission of such crimes is criminal battery or sexual assault, not civil disorderly conduct. To refer such cases for civil prosecution merely gives batterers a wrong impression—namely, that they truly are free to abuse their mates and that nobody in the system will take such abuse seriously, protect their abused mates, or hold them criminally liable for their misconduct. That's not justice.

8. Judges and Sentencing

Prosecutors make recommendations to judges regarding appropriate sentences for persons who commit crimes. Defense attorneys object to such sentences, unless a plea agreement has been reached. Prosecutors need to recommend and push for serious jail terms (sometimes with work release privileges) for persons who commit acts of domestic abuse—in the same way they would unquestionably push for serious jail terms for persons who batter or sexually assault strangers. This is necessary to hold batterers accountable for their misconduct, and to give them the clear message that it is not acceptable to abuse their mates. Judges, in turn, have to take domestic violence cases seriously, and to issue appropriately severe jail terms to men or women who have domestically abused their mates.

It is inappropriate, in this author's view, for prosecutors to plea bargain with batterers and their attorneys to seriously reduce or drop charges of domestic abuse. Such plea bargains are typical in our system (which never has enough prosecutors, police, courts, support staff, etc. to hold a lot of trials). Justice, however, dictates that plea bargains which permit domestic abusers to escape appropriate punishment for their crimes not be made or agreed to by prosecutors. Prosecutors have a duty to stand up for the best interests of the victims of crime. It is not in a domestic abuse victim's best interest to have the charges against her or his abuser dropped or greatly reduced to a minor offense.

9. Reforming the Criminal Justice System

Prosecutors, in their critical role in the criminal justice system, have a duty to the public whom they serve, and toward the victims of crime whom they help, to actively push for reforms within the system which are necessary to improve the handling of domestic abuse cases. The needed reforms will vary from jurisdiction to jurisdiction. However, among the most obvious examples of reforms which may be needed are: more prosecutorial staff; more judges; more space; more jail cells; more counselors for abuse victims; more shelters for safety of victims; tougher sentencing by judges faced by domestic abuse cases; better financial aid and child care for victims of abuse; more police officers; better training of police, prosecutors, social workers, and other professionals who deal with domestic abuse cases; etc. Prosecutors must take a serious look at how the criminal justice system in their communities is functioning to help victims of domestic abuse. Weak spots in the networking system should be pinpointed and fixed. Needed funds should be sought from legislatures, and other funding sources. Law changes should be considered and pushed for.

Prosecutors, clearly, play a major role in the appropriate resolution of domestic abuse cases in our society. They must, in fairness, and in the interests of equal treatment of crime victims and justice in our society, take such cases as seriously as they take other nondomestic crimes.

Chapter 13

WHAT TO DO WHEN HE WON'T LEAVE

A major problem faced by many victims of domestic abuse is how to keep their abusers from continuing to contact them, harass them, abuse them, and make their lives miserable—after they, as victims, have decided to end the relationship.

Batterers have a tendency to refuse to leave the woman they abused alone. This problem can lead to a continuation of the abuse, unless effectively thwarted by the joint efforts of the abused woman and the legal system.

Most batterers will come back. Even if the mate they abused makes it clear that she does not want to have any contact with him anymore. Even if the man is under a court order not to have contact with the woman. Many of these men will show up at the homes of their abused ex-mates. Perhaps it was the home they shared. That's one reason why some women go to shelters for a while. Batterers tend to make harassing phone calls to their victims. Many threaten to commit suicide if the mate won't take them back. This, and other manipulative behavior, such as promising to change their behavior, and claiming to love their victims, often persuades victims to take these men back into their lives. And nothing changes.

It takes a very strong, self-confident woman to stand up to a batterer's attempts to continue the relationship. Unfortunately, abused women tend to lack such self-esteem. Battered women often fall for the batterers' psychological ploys or fall victim to their use of physical force to remain in the women's lives.

As a result, it becomes critical that the legal system function effectively to help battered women to keep their abusers out of their lives.

The primary method used by our system of justice to help battered women keep their abusers away from them is what is known as a domestic abuse restraining order.

To obtain a domestic abuse restraining order, a woman must claim in a petition to the court that the person whom she seeks a restraining order against abused her, physically, in some way. Details of the abuse should be given in the petition. Help should be sought from domestic abuse center workers or whatever agency helps victims draft such orders in the community where the victim lives. In Wisconsin, for example, only allegations of physical abuse (hitting, choking, kicking, shooting, cutting with a knife, beating, shoving, etc.) will qualify a victim for a domestic abuse restraining order. If a case involves emotional abuse and/or harassment alone, a victim may be able to get a harassment restraining order which will, effectively, also serve to keep the abuser away from her. It is advisable to put as much detail about various incidents of abuse into these petitions as possible in order to convince the judge who will determine whether or not to approve the petition to do so.

Temporary restraining orders are issued based on the word of the victim, as set forth in the petition, without having to give legal notice to the abuser. However, these orders will last for only a short period of time, usually up to a couple of weeks at most. A victim must be informed of this fact and be prepared for the worst possible scenario, namely, for the batterer to object to the restraining order being made permanent (for a couple of years). Many abusers will deny having abused the victim and will object to a restraining order being issued against them. Therefore, many women who obtain temporary orders will wind up having to go into court to testify, under oath, about their abuse at a hearing on making the order permanent. By the time these hearings occur, unfortunately, many abused women have already given in to their abusers' demands (in violation of the temporary orders) to take them back into their lives. Therefore, these women will fail to show up for the hearing and the orders wind up not being made permanent.

An effective support system for an abused woman, consisting of a battered woman center or other abuse program counselor/advocate, and, perhaps a close friend or family member, can help to give the woman the strength to go through with the injunction hearing and to get a permanent order. It is very hard for battered women to talk about their abuse in public (because it is such a private thing which they have hidden from others for lengthy periods of time). Their support person(s) should help them to prepare to answer the judge's questions regarding the abuse set forth in the petition, and, in some cases, prepare to answer unfriendly cross-examination-style questions from an attorney for the abuser. They must also be prepared to hear the batterer deny that the abuse took place, even under oath in court. Preparing to face the abuser in court is also a very difficult task which support persons should caution battered women to expect. Batterers do not give up what they consider their right to abuse their mates easily.

Courtrooms where domestic disputes are heard should be made safe by devices such as metal detectors and, if appropriate, stationing of police/sheriff's deputies in the courtroom to preserve order and prevent possible violence. This author makes this recommendation in light of numerous tragedies around the nation in public buildings involving volatile domestic disputes/divorces/custody matters.

In this author's opinion, two major factors enter into the failure by some domestic abuse victims to obtain temporary restraining orders or, if they obtain one of those, to follow through with the process of obtaining a permanent restraining order. The first is FEAR. These women fear that their abuser may abuse them worse if they testify against them, get a restraining order, or cooperate in prosecuting them for battery or other crimes. These fears are realistic. However, there is also no doubt that in almost all of these cases, the failure to take steps to stop the abuse (restraining orders, arrest and prosecution, or successful completion of a batterers' program) is a guarantee that the abuse will continue. I would, therefore, argue, that women who are abused should take the chance that their taking action to stop the abuse will be effective. We already know that the failure to act guarantees future abuse. The second factor is the fact that the women "love" the abusers. This issue was dealt with at length in Chapter 4 and will not be repeated here. This "love" for the abuser, the fear of being alone, the symptoms of the battered woman syndrome, the cycle theory of violence, and, the general behavior patterns and attitudes of battered women, play a major role in preventing some of these women from accepting the help the system offers them in the form of the chance to obtain a domestic abuse restraining order. That is why it is so critical that the persons within the system (cops, social workers, battered woman center staff, prosecutors, counselors, etc.) who are responsible for helping battered women to end their abuse network effectively together to persuade such women to accept their help, and take actions to help these women through the system.

Problems Concerning Restraining Orders

Various problems exist concerning restraining orders which professionals, victims, and the public need to be made aware of. These include:

1. Some judges are reluctant to grant such orders. The point to be made is different standards of "justice" exist across the nation, and even from community to community within each state, in the handling and acceptance of petitions for restraining orders. The way such petitions are treated often depends upon the personal value system of the judge before whom the restraining order petition is brought. Judges who understand what abuse victims experience and who are sympathetic to their plights are far more willing to cooperate in issuing such injunctions than are judges who still suffer from the attitude that domestic violence is not a crime and is a "family" matter which does not belong in the criminal justice system. One way for advocates on behalf of battered women who are wrongly denied restraining orders to challenge such outcomes might be to appeal a judge's order to a higher court.

2. The domestic abuse victims often (unless they have appropriate moral support from the advocates, shelters, or friends) fail to take the steps necessary to make temporary restraining orders permanent. The reasons for this were set forth above.

3. The petitions for restraining orders must be drafted sufficiently in order to enable a judge to grant an order. Many victims may have difficulty figuring out how to write such a petition. It is important for communities to have domestic abuse center advocates or other skilled persons available to help battered women write their petitions. One problem, for example, may occur if a woman fails to allege that physical abuse took place—and lists only verbal threats or putdowns or emotional abuse in her petition. That may not, at least in some places, be sufficient to obtain a restraining order. The history of abuse, including incidents prior to the one which led to the victim's contact with the system, should be detailed in the petition.

4. Many women feel they will be in more danger if they obtain a restraining order, or take other action against the abuser, than if they tolerate the abuse. The reasons why this attitude is held by abused women, and why it is an inaccurate attitude were discussed above.

5. A restraining order must be placed on file with appropriate law enforcement agencies in order for those agencies to be able to arrest a batterer who violates an order—or the woman must be able to provide the order to police after a violation occurs. The police will not arrest an abuser for violating an order unless they are presented with a copy of the order. Advocates for battered women should see that such orders are

filed with law enforcement agencies immediately after they are signed by the judge.

6. The failure of police officers to enforce restraining orders (i.e., failure to arrest persons who violate them) is a major problem in many communities. This brings us back to the entire issue of the need to sensitize police officers to the seriousness of domestic violence and of our system to require law enforcement to cooperate in efforts to keep batterers away from the women they have abused. If a batterer gets away with violating an order which states that he is to have no contact (physical or verbal) with the mate he abused, he is likely to ignore the order. If, however, police arrest him for violating the order, he is more likely to avoid violating it in the future.

7. Some prosecutors fail to prosecute abusers who violate domestic abuse restraining orders. This should not be the case. A batterer who fails to be prosecuted for violating the order is likely to violate it again. Prosecutors need to be committed to fighting domestic abuse by enforcing such restraining orders—in order to ensure the future safety of the battered women who have obtained such orders.

8. Victims of domestic abuse frequently violate their own restraining orders by contacting the abuser. The author realizes this sounds absurd. It frequently occurs. Most restraining orders prohibit both the batterer and his victim from having any physical (in-person) or verbal (even over the phone) contact with each other. Therefore, if the female who is the victim of abuse and obtained the order goes to see the batterer, or phones him, or invites him over, *she* is in violation of the order, and is also subject to arrest. This needs to be explained to abuse victims by the domestic abuse center advocates and the judge at the time they obtain restraining orders. The reasons why battered women tend to contact their abusers are many, again related to their attitudes and behavior as battered women. Their dependency on the abuser, their own lack of self-esteem and inability to function on their own, and their love for him are among the key factors which may lead them to contact the abuser. Also important are financial needs and issues of visitation concerning children. It is frequently necessary to ensure that the woman's financial needs are being met (by court orders for child support or alimony, or public aid) and that a method of visitation which avoids contact of any sort between the victim and the abuser is established by a court. (In some cases, visitation is inappropriate, such as when a child has also been abused.)

9. The sorts of human relationships we are dealing with in domestic situations are so charged with emotions (love; hate; obsession; jealousy; happiness; sadness; depression; etc.) that such cases are difficult to successfully resolve. Restraining order issues become part of the entire issue of resolution of the disputes between the parties.

10. Restraining orders and even arrest for violations of such orders are ineffective against the worst, most obsessively jealous batterers. This presents a major problem because police protection of women on a frequent basis is usually not possible—even in states where such victim's rights appear to be guaranteed by state constitutions or by statute. Some women have been forced to deal with this problem by moving far away and changing their identities. These are the kinds of situations where a serious potential of severe injury or death to one of the parties exists. Short of locking up such batterers for substantial periods of time, there seems to be no reliable solution to these extra dangerous situations. It must be emphasized that the criminal justice system must do what it can to ensure the safety of domestic abuse victims.

CONCLUSION

Our legal system must do everything in its power to help battered women end the abuse in their lives.

Equally important, we must also do whatever we can to help abuse victims find the inner strength to keep their abusers out of their lives, or, where appropriate, the strength to force their abusers to change their pattern of abuse and begin to treat them decently.

Chapter 14

PARDON ME: DEATH FROM
DOMESTIC VIOLENCE

The most tragic of all domestic abuse cases are those which end in the death of the abused woman or the abusive man.

This chapter addresses the following topics which relate to domestic violence cases which result in death:

Example of a domestic violence death.
Why battered women kill.
Self-defense issues.
Gubernatorial pardons.

The author's book, *Representing ... Battered Women Who Kill*, should be consulted for defense strategies in defending battered women who kill their abuser against homicide charges, and for more data on such cases.

Example of a Case Which Results in the Death of the Abuser

The author of this book has consulted in cases of battered women who killed their abuser, and has studied many more cases where such deaths occurred. As a result, she is aware of the thinking, experiences, and sorts of incidents which lead some battered women to fight back against abuse by killing their abuser. Rather than using any specific victim's case, and risk violating client confidentiality, the author has chosen to create for the reader a fictitious example of a battered woman who killed her abuser in order to help the reader understand what causes such women to kill in self-defense. The fictitious account below is written in the first person to make it more realistic.

Prelude to Death

The abuse got so bad, so unbearable, that I began to daydream about what it would be like for my children and me to exist in a world without *him* in it. Without my husband. My children's father.

It would be tranquil.

Peaceful.

I would not have to live with the constant fear that he will kill me. That next time he abuses me, chokes me, holds a knife to my throat, or a gun to my head he will actually follow through on his threats to kill me.

I daydream about killing him.

Lighting a match and torching our bed while he is asleep in it.

Poisoning his food. That would serve him right. Pay him back for all the times he hit me because he did not like a meal I'd made.

I consider buying a handgun. But I wouldn't even know how to use it. Where to aim the gun. I don't think I'd be capable of harming an animal, let alone shooting a human being.

I'd like to shoot him in the balls. To make sure he could never rape or sexually abuse me again.

One time he took a gun and held it to my vagina—and threatened to pull the trigger.

I believed he could do it.

Another time he got so furious with me for getting pregnant again—as if it was all *my* fault—that he aborted our child with a coat hanger, and nearly killed me in the process, too.

I'm still experiencing emotional problems as a result.

I don't believe in abortion.

I told the doctor about this. When he treated me for an infection.

He didn't believe me.

Neither did the cops. My friend insisted I call them.

In all the times I called the cops, they never arrested my husband for abuse.

Despite my bruises.

Even though my neighbor lady told them I was telling the truth. She overheard me screaming at Andrew, my husband, begging him not to hit me. And saw my bruises when I came out of the house after she called the cops. The police took statements. Andrew ran off before they arrived.

They did nothing to help me.

Andrew came back. He was even more intoxicated than before.

He raped me that night. He knew the rape would be painful, but it would not leave any marks, any proof of abuse.

Andrew likes to strike me with an old worn-out leather belt, after tying me down to the bed with ropes, to make me helpless, and submissive.

I never told anybody about this.

I figured no one would believe me. I was too embarrassed about this to even tell my mom or my sister or my friends.

More recently I have begun to live in terror that he will abuse the kids. Molest our daughter.

He's been making remarks lately about how pretty and how grown up she's getting. Sometimes he says he'll enjoy having her to have relations with after he's gotten rid of me.

I hope he's joking.

Ann, our daughter, is only 11. She looks 14. Sexy. Like kids do these days. He's bought her sexy clothing to wear.

Andrew has been reading those incest pornography magazines and books, and watching incest-movies, all of which promote incest and sex with minors. This scares me. I'm scared for my daughter. I'm scared he might touch her in some improper way.

I don't like the way he's been looking at Ann lately. He always used to look at me that way, sort of like he was trying to be seductive, when we were dating. He looks at me that way now when he wants to engage in sex.

Common sense tells me that he wouldn't actually molest our own child.

Would he?

My uncertainty bothers me.

My own childhood is a blur. I suppose I may have been molested. I just don't remember much of anything about my early years. Except for being shy and scared all the time.

Until Andrew entered my life. In my high school years. He seemed like the perfect mate, the perfect way for me to get out of my parents' house, to find a life of my own. He was so nice, caring, considerate, loving. Love was something I wasn't used to experiencing.

The summer after we graduated from high school, Andrew and I began to be sexually intimate. I got pregnant with our daughter Ann. We got married at age 18. We were just kids, unprepared for the shock of the real world, too immature to raise a family.

Andrew has stood by me through the years. I give him credit for that.

Except his cheating on me—with other women—breaks my heart. He claims these "flings" mean nothing to him. That it's me he loves. Not Cheryl. Or Christine. Or Deborah. I feel so bad when he does this. Like I'm just not good enough for him.

I still love him. I always will.

I'd be lost without him. Completely helpless.

Andrew has been frightening me more than usual lately. He is becoming more violent, more angry, more dangerous. At least it seems that way to me.

I fear for my life.

Last month he picked up a hot frying pan full of grease and threw it at me. It hit my arm, burning me. The hot grease splashed on my neck and arms and burned me in numerous spots.

Our son Drew witnessed this. He's only 8, but he tried to intervene. Andrew threw him against a cabinet and he bumped his forehead. I'm surprised nobody from his school asked him how he got hurt. I guess they assumed he was just a kid who hurt himself roughhousing with other kids. Andrew didn't even seem to care that he had hurt his own son.

I'm afraid Andrew might injure Drew again. In one of his fits of rage.

I still think he may have been trying to drown Drew when he "accidentally" slipped beneath the bathtub water when he gave him a bath when he was a year old. Luckily I came into the room. In time to see him pull Drew out of the water. He claimed he slipped and slid under the water. I've always wondered about that.

A couple of times the police brought Andrew home after he participated in drunken brawls at taverns. He got prosecuted for cutting a man's head open with a broken beer bottle.

He cut my hand with a knife a few months ago.

Nobody prosecuted him for that. He claimed I had cut myself while peeling potatoes.

Did the police and prosecutor believe him because he's a small businessman and I'm a housewife?

Andrew said next time I wouldn't be so lucky. He said he would cut my throat. And held one of those big butcher knives to my throat to emphasize the point.

I cannot put into words how terrified I was.

I still have nightmares that he will kill me.

I truly believe he will someday.

Unless I kill him first.

I'd never be able to do that.

He's too strong. Physically. I wouldn't stand a chance against his strength.

I couldn't hurt anybody anyway. I am not violent.

I truly believe I would let him kill me first.

Lately he's been cleaning and fiddling with his hunting rifles.

He tells me that this year he's not planning to go hunting for deer. He says he's going to hunt and kill me instead.

Surely he's joking.

I'm never quite sure.

When he looks at me out of those cold, unfeeling eyes, I shiver.

A couple days ago he pointed a rifle at me.

And pulled the trigger.

It was not loaded.

He laughed. And laughed. Like a madman.

At my fear. At my tears. At my pleas for him to stop terrorizing me, and my pleas to let me live.

He said next time the rifle will be loaded. From the way he looked at me, I'm convinced he's insane enough to do it.

I am so afraid he'll kill me.

Sometimes I think I would be better off dead.

There would be no more abuse.

But I have to think of the children. I can't leave them alone with him.

After he put the rifle away, he subjected me to a night of sexual abuse. I am still in pain from the humiliating things he did to me.

If this is "love" what is "hate"?

I don't know how much more abuse I can tolerate.

Maybe I should kill myself. To end the abuse.

I tried that once.

And failed.

I didn't swallow enough sleeping pills.

Not surprising. I've been a failure at everything all my life.

He keeps telling me that.

When he beats me.

The beatings have gotten worse lately.

They started soon after we were married while I was pregnant with our daughter Ann. He hit me in the stomach a couple of times. I was so afraid I would lose the baby. He said that's what he wanted.

He likes to strike me in the arms and shoulders with his fist. This always leaves bruises. Which I cover up by wearing long-sleeved shirts and dresses.

I actually got the nerve to hit him back. Twice. He just laughed at me.

And hit me in the face with his fist. One time I thought he had broken my nose.

He caused me to break my leg. He shoved me down the basement stairs.

He left me lying there, at the bottom of the stairs, to suffer. Our son, then 6, found me. The doctor doubted my story about having fallen down the stairs. I refused to tell him the truth. Andrew had threatened to kill me if I told anybody. I believed him. I did not tell.

Andrew has tried to kill me a few times.

Once, when he had me tied down during sex play, he wrapped a nylon stocking around my neck and choked me. He kept it up so long that I passed out. When I woke up he acted like nothing had happened.

Then there were the times when he held guns to my head and knives to my throat.

I was terrified that he really would kill me.

He held a gun to my head again last night. And said he intended to kill me with it during the night while I slept.

When I looked up into his face, and saw the expression there, I knew that he truly intended to kill me this time. I believed him.

I thought I was going to die.

And I did not want to die.

The Killing

Something in me must have snapped last night.

They tell me that I shot Andrew with his pistol. When his back was turned.

I don't remember doing that.

I don't remember it at all.

The police say they found me sitting in a rocking chair beside his body, holding the pistol in my lap. They claim I called 911 and screamed hysterically in the phone that I had shot my husband. And that I had his blood all over my clothes.

I really don't know what happened.

I'm not sure I want to know.

It all seems so unreal. Like a dream. A nightmare.

I just don't remember anything.

The Arrest

I think I'm in real trouble now.

I'm in the county jail.

The cops arrested me.

They think I murdered Andrew. I don't know if I did it.

I never intended to kill him. I just wanted to stop the abuse. I wanted to prevent him from killing me. I knew he was going to.

I think he's still alive. He must be alive.

They're lying to me about Andrew being dead.

What Would Happen to a Woman Who Killed Her Abusive Mate?

Scenario A

The short answer to the question of what should happen to a woman who kills her abusive mate (perhaps in a situation similar to that of the fictitious account presented above) is *nothing*.

In a properly-functioning criminal justice system, the woman who killed her husband in self-defense under the type of circumstances described:

1. Would not be arrested for the killing.

2. Police and prosecutors would investigate the circumstances of the killing and determine that the killing was justifiable because it was done in self-defense.

3. Counseling and other help from domestic abuse experts would be provided to the woman.

If the police arrest, the prosecutor wrongly prosecutes the woman for first degree murder, manslaughter, or some other criminal charge:

A. The woman should obtain an attorney who specializes in cases of battered women who kill their abuser.

B. The attorney would use expert witnesses to detail the Battered Woman syndrome (after having had her/his client examined to determine that she suffered from the syndrome and obtaining a history of abuse from her), and to explain why such women kill in self-defense. Or, it might also be argued, or argued as an alternative, that the woman suffered from a mental disease or defect at the time of the killing (such as the Borderline Personality Disorder or the Posttraumatic Stress Disorder).

C. Upon being presented with the evidence of abuse the judge would dismiss the case against the woman, or the jury would recognize that she killed her abuser in self-defense and acquit her.

D. If the rest of the system fails the woman, the governor of the state should pardon her.

The system would be functioning as it should only in the situation where the authorities would investigate the killing, determine that it was justified, and not arrest or prosecute the woman.

Scenario B

In an improperly-functioning criminal justice system, which still describes most jurisdictions in our nation, this woman, who killed an abusive mate in self-defense, would be wrongly arrested, prosecuted, and found guilty of first degree murder or manslaughter, tossed in a state prison for women, and forgotten by all except the children, family, and friends who love her and understand the injustice of what the system did to her.

The truth is, we live in a nation that unjustly arrests, prosecutes, convicts, and imprisons hundreds of women yearly who fight back against unbearable and dangerous abuse by their mates in the only realistic way they can (because the system has failed them)—by killing their abusers. They join thousands of other women who have already been wrongly convicted and are wrongly in prisons across the nation for similar offenses. In reality, these women have not committed any crime and were wrongly charged, tried, and convicted by an unjust system which continues to promote the domestic and sexual abuse of women and wrongly attacks women who finally exercise their constitutional right (to life, liberty) to defend themselves from likely death or severe bodily harm.

In this unfair system, the following sorts of things are likely to happen to a battered woman who kills her abuser:

1. She will be interrogated by police with no attorney present and confess to having killed her mate—but the system will decide that the confession was "voluntary" although it was not.

2. She will fail to tell her attorney (if she or he fails to ask whether she was abused) and she will fail to tell authorities why she killed her mate, namely that she was an abused woman. Her attorney may or may not be aware that she should be examined by an expert in domestic violence homicide cases as soon as possible after the killing to determine whether she was an abused woman who killed in self-defense or while under the influence of a mental disease or defect. In fact, so many women who kill

their mates do so because they have been victimized and abused by them that any attorney or authority faced by a case of a woman who kills a mate should be trained to and should investigate the likelihood that this was the reason for the killing.

3. She will be wrongly arrested, tried for, and convicted of first degree murder, or manslaughter, or perhaps even a lesser offense, and given an unfairly long prison term.

4. She may be unable to afford legal counsel who specializes in cases of battered women who kill (most attorneys avoid these cases because many of these women don't have much money). She may also be unable to afford the fees of the expert witnesses she needs to investigate her case, evaluate her, and testify in court about her suffering from the Battered Woman syndrome. Some courts may be unwilling to pay the fees of such experts although such homicide defendants are unable to properly defend themselves without such testimony/expert consultants. Such experts are needed to persuade a jury that she killed in self-defense and committed no crime, and to help the jury understand why her behavior differs from how they would, logically, expect someone who is battered or abused to behave.

5. The prosecutor will try to keep the truth about the woman's abuse from being told to the jury because it will explain why she killed, and justify the killing as being in self-defense.

6. The prosecutor will try to prevent expert testimony about the Battered Woman syndrome and/or other expert explanations about why the women behaved as she did from being heard by the jury. (Most states allow such testimony; a few don't.)

7. The judge is unlikely, unfortunately, to dismiss the criminal charges against the woman at a preliminary hearing (into whether there was probable cause that she committed the so-called crime). (This is another stage at which informed and competent defense counsel would seek to get the case dismissed.)

8. The governor is unlikely to pardon these women.

Readers of this book may ask why such travesties of justice occur hundreds of times a year in America. I suggest that it is for the same reason that domestic abuse batteries do not show up as "crimes" in the F.B.I. annual criminal statistics, and are not added in as "crimes" by local or state authorities. The "system" does not take these cases seriously. While its representatives tend to talk about domestic violence cases as tragedies, and crimes, the criminal justice system, in reality, still treats these cases as "family" matters, not the crimes against real women, real crime victims, that they truly are. The reasons for this incompetent and improper handling of cases involving domestic crimes against women were set forth in Chapter 6.

Case outcomes which result in battered women who kill their abusers in self-defense being arrested, prosecuted, convicted, and imprisoned, are clearly unjust. Yet our society allows this tragedy to happen to hundreds of women a year in our nation. We must actively fight to change this, along with fighting to prevent the domestic violence incidents from escalating to the point where one party kills the other.

Why Some Battered Women Kill Their Abusers

The simple answer to the question of why some battered women kill their abusers is that they do so in self-defense. The self-defense issue becomes a very complex one, legally, as the nation's laws on self-defense were written to justify men killing other men in certain types of cases, and do not take into account relevant differences in self-defense issues which occur when a woman kills a man in self-defense. This author, in her prior book, *Representing...Battered Women Who Kill,* and in this work, continues to take the position that self-defense laws must be formally rewritten across our nation to take such differences into account.

The reality is that it is foolish for our criminal justice system to attempt to apply the same self-defense standards to most men and women. The truth is that most women are not trained in fighting/combat/defensive tactics as children the way many boys/men are; most women are not as strong, physically, as most men; and most women would need a gun, knife, or other weapon to successfully defend against a battery or sexual assault by most men. The only way that most battered women would be able to defend themselves against the continual threat of death or other serious bodily harm their abuser holds over them is by fighting back in self-defense against the abuser when his back is turned or when he is asleep. That, in reality, is exactly what happens in the situations of many battered women who kill their abuser. They kill them in self-defense at a moment when the abuser has momentarily stopped abusing them, or turned his back, or gone to sleep. However, these women are still acting in self-defense because they are under a constant threat of death or serious injury from their abuser. Our nation's self-defense laws need to be reformed to take relevant differences in the ability of men and women to defend themselves into account (while, obviously, allowing for exceptions to be made if specific case facts do not fit the standard pattern, for example if a man who is small, untrained in self-defense or combat, and weak, defends himself against a woman who is tall, strong, and has military training in combat techniques). Those laws should also spell out how self-defense in cases of battered women who kill their abuser differs from standard self-defense situations.

A lot of men grow up believing that part of their cultural role is to protect and care for women. Some people reject such a concept as sexist.

I believe there is a vast difference between sexism which denies women equal job opportunities, shared child care/home responsibilities, equal education, equal wages, equal pay for work of comparable value, equal political power, and equal say in decision-making in life (in the home and the community)—and men protecting women from physical danger and treating them with courtesy, and caring for their needs.

If we say there's something wrong with men being caring, protective, and gentlemanly toward women, we're saying we approve of them being assaultive, combative, rough, and tough and macho. The point is that we, as human beings, all need to treat each other with respect, nicely, kindly, protectively, and caringly. It doesn't matter if we're talking about a woman interacting with a man, or vice versa, or women interacting with women or men interacting with men. The tough, rough, combative, angry, fight about differences of opinion rather than resolve them verbally, attitude does a great deal of damage in relationships and society. Violence is not an answer to anybody's problems. Understanding, peaceful attempts to resolve differences, kindness, helpfulness, and concern for fellow human beings are the answers. Until we, as a society, stop tolerating violence and start promoting peace, our social problems are destined to get worse and worse and worse.

This author sees nothing wrong with a man having a protective, gentlemanly attitude and behavior pattern toward women. In fact, that sort of behavior and attitude can be a major way for a man to express his "love" to a woman in his life. A man who feels that way toward his mate would not batter or otherwise abuse her. Having respect for, and caring for another person will improve, not harm, a domestic relationship.

Battered women kill their abusers when their sense of imminent deadly danger toward their children or themselves reaches a point where they (usually correctly) believe the batterer will kill them or their children if they don't kill him first.

When battered women kill, it is in self-defense (even in situations like those where the woman sets the man's bed on fire while he is asleep or shoots him when his back is turned). The only time when a battered woman will typically be able to stand a chance of defending herself against an abuser's intentions to kill her is when he is asleep or when his back is turned, and/or by using a weapon like a gun or knife rather than her hands.

Some people may argue that these cases appear, on the surface, to be intentional homicides. They are not. When a battered woman finally fights back against an abuser in self-defense with serious force, she *rarely* has any intent to kill him. She merely is acting in self-defense to stop him from killing or seriously injuring her or her children. Even when battered women kill an abuser, they usually refuse to believe he is actually dead because they truly do not believe they can harm him. So, *intent* to kill is truly not present in these cases.

Some battered women who kill also suffer from a mental disease such as Borderline Personality syndrome or Posttraumatic Stress Disorder. I believe the Battered Woman syndrome (which battered women suffer from) deserves its own place in psychological theories, rather than continuing to remain a sociological theory of behavior, and that it will someday be classified as a mental disorder in psychological terms. It is this syndrome, and its characteristics, as experienced by real women in real cases which helps professionals to understand why some battered women kill their abuser in self-defense.

Battered women kill because our criminal and civil "justice" systems have failed to protect them from the abusive mates. Most cases where such women kill have a long history of police refusing to arrest abusers, or prosecutors failing to prosecute these criminals, and a failure of the system to provide protection to the women, or to take steps to force the batterer to reform his behavior (such as by batterer programs). When the system fails to help a battered woman, it risks her being murdered by the batterer or her having to kill the batterer in self-defense.

Battered Women Who Kill: Self-Defense Issues

In doing the research for and writing *Representing...Battered Women Who Kill,* this author read, summarized, and drew conclusions from dozens of professional articles and books dealing with the topic of self-defense issues in cases involving battered women who kill their abuser.

Readers should be aware that this extensive data base is available to those who wish to do further research into this area. *Representing . . . Battered Women Who Kill* cites many of these articles and books in its extensive bibliography. The following description of the complex issues surrounding self-defense considerations in cases of battered women who kill their abuser is taken from Chapter 3 of that book:

> Self-defense is the defense used in most battered women who kill cases. Most self-defense laws have three requirements:
>
> 1. A person may only use armed force against unlawful armed force (proportionality or equal force rule).
>
> 2. The attack victim must reasonably fear the danger is imminent or immediate.
>
> 3. The victim must seek any avenue of retreat before using defensive force.
>
> In addition, the attack must have been unprovoked. Generally, words or threats don't, by themselves, justify taking another's life. . . .
>
> Many problems arise in attempting to apply traditional self-defense standards to battered women who kill. For example, if a "reasonable man" standard is applied, the woman may not be able to successfully meet that requirement. The defense must encourage use of a "reasonable battered woman" or "reasonable woman" standard instead. The states are split on whether self-defense standards should apply objective or subjective rules. The objective standard looks at the self-defense claim from the perspective of the reasonable man. For example, to apply the objective standard to the element of a defendant's belief that she was in imminent danger of unlawful bodily harm, the defendant must have believed self-defense was necessary and that belief must have been reasonable by the standards of the ordinary person. The subjective standard (the one that defense attorneys should seek in these types of cases) looks at the claim from the perceptions of the particular individual. Under this test, the fact that the defendant's belief was unreasonable, won't defeat the claim. In battered women who kill cases, it is critical that the reasonableness standard be extended to assume the fears and weaknesses of the defendant, or of the battered woman, and that the self-defense issue be looked at from the perspective of what action would have been reasonable, under the circumstances, for a typical battered woman. This is where admission of Battered Woman syndrome testimony becomes critical, for it can help the judge or jury understand the battered woman's perspective.
>
> The equal force requirement of self-defense laws also becomes a major issue in battered woman who kill cases, for often the woman uses lethal force (a gun or knife) against a man who attacked her with his hands or who is sleeping or has his back turned at the time of the killing. Here it must be argued that women in general, and the woman in the particular case, must use lethal force in order to defend against men in general and the particular man due to differences in size, strength and use of force training. . . .
>
> The traditional self-defense requirement that the threat of harm be immi-

nent or immediate frequently causes problems for the defense in attempting to make battered women who kill fit such theories. The men who were killed were often attacked by these women when they were sleeping or their backs were turned and they did not appear to be posing an immediate or imminent threat to the women. The defense must utilize BWS testimony to show a jury why the defendant perceived "imminent" danger in a situation where someone other than a battered woman would not. Emphasis should be put on the fact that these women are sensitive to cues of impending assault by their batterers. We suggest the defense present (through an expert) the theory of cumulative terror or murder by installment. Argue that the man was murdering the woman on an installment basis and that she knew future violence was certain. . . . Thus, her perception of an imminent or immediate threat was very real. When the woman kills in response to an immediate attack by the batterer or an imminent threat by him such arguments may not be needed. . . .

Sarah Baseden Vandenbraak (1979) calls for a more flexible self-defense standard embodying "the principle that an actor's use of force is justified only if he reasonably believes that such force is necessary to prevent unlawful harm." She explained that this makes necessity the ultimate issue. It eliminates imminence or immediacy requirements and does not impose a duty to retreat. . . . (47–49)

This author believes that imminence or immediacy should indeed be eliminated as an element of self-defense, and that it is clear that battered women should have no duty to retreat from their own home (in order to avoid having to defend themselves from potential death or serious harm). Nothing short of some sort of successful effort to change the behavior of batterers (to end their abuse) is going to remove battered women from the constant terror and constant danger they face of being killed or seriously injured by their abusers. When a handful of these women act to prevent their own deaths or serious injury at the hands of their mates each year, we, as a society, must not blame them for taking the only actions they could to protect themselves and/or their children. Instead of arresting, prosecuting, and wrongly jailing these women (who have committed no crime), we should concentrate our efforts on reforming the criminal justice system to eliminate the need for battered women to kill their abusers in self-defense.

Pardon Me

The author of this book firmly believes that the governors of the 50 states should take active steps to investigate all individual cases of women who are in their state prisons for having killed their mates to determine which of these women were battered and killed in self-defense or while under the influence of a mental disease or defect (caused by the battering). The governors should then pardon all women whom they determine are in prison and fit that category of inmates. Some governors have done this.

The letter which follows is a fictional one written from the perspective of a battered woman who killed an abuser to the governor of her state.

Dear Governor:

I sit in my cell at the women's state prison, staring at the four walls that imprison me.

And think of how much safer I am here than I was when I lived imprisoned in the constant state of terror that my husband kept me in in our own home. I lived with the constant fear that he would kill me. Or our children.

I am in prison because I finally killed him.

In self-defense. After years of physical, sexual, and emotional abuse.

I honestly believed he was going to murder me on the night I killed him.

He tried to kill me a few times before. And threatened to do so much more often.

I believed him.

On the night when I shot him he told me he planned to kill me after I fell asleep.

I was terrified.

I still believe he would have killed me that night.

They tell me I killed him instead.

I never intended to kill him. I just wanted to keep him from killing me and my children that very night.

When he looked at me the way he did that night—with that cold, hateful, dangerous expression in his eyes—I knew I had to injure him to keep him from killing me and our kids.

I guess I thought if I injured him somebody would finally believe me, would finally help me to stop the abuse.

They arrested and prosecuted me instead.

My attorney, the psychologist who examined me and said I suffered from the Battered Woman syndrome and a Borderline Personality Disorder and who testified on my behalf at trial, the witnesses to my abuse who told the truth on the witness stand, and my friends and family members tell me that I was justified in killing my husband. That I deserve your pardon. That I had no other choice, no other way to prevent him from killing me and/or our kids. I know I acted in self-defense.

But I will never forgive myself for killing him.

I understand now why I did what I did. My attorney, the psychologist, the people who supported me from the local battered woman center, explained it to me.

Can you understand that I had no choice?

If I hadn't shot him he would have killed me and/or my children.

I am not a bad person.

A killer.

A criminal.

Please pardon me, Governor. So that I can go home, be with my children who need me, and try to start a new life.

Chapter 15

DESTRUCTION OF THE FAMILY UNIT

We must be greatly concerned, as a society, that the result of the domestic and other abuse running rampant in our nation, has been to destroy the family as a unit. It becomes obvious that the only way to put a halt to the tremendous number of divorces, and to encourage intimate partners to marry (instead of living together) is to bring about a major change of attitude and behavior on the part of the numerous individuals who have abused their mates. Until we are able to change this attitude and behavior pattern, the breakup of families will continue to spiral, with the resultant social problems it creates, such as juvenile delinquency, poverty, and emotional problems for the women who are left alone to raise the children, huge medical costs, loss of work productivity, a heightened demand for social services and criminal justice system services, and the like.

Our failure, as a country, to effectively prevent and stop domestic violence has consequences far beyond the immediate impact of the abuse.

Too many domestic violence incidents end in the death or serious injury of the victim or the abuser. Children are left homeless.

This author is highly concerned about the breakup of families in America. The consequence of this is that too many children are growing up inappropriately in single-parent homes (usually with the mother), or in foster homes. These children are being taught that to be a male in our culture is to be able to avoid responsibility, to live a free and easy do as you please lifestyle, and to be free to abuse women and children without being held accountable by the family or the criminal justice system. This is tragic.

Properly caring for a child is difficult enough under normal living conditions (in which the mother, father, and children reside in the same home). This task becomes far more difficult for a single parent who needs an emotional bond with a mate (in order to be emotionally and psychologically secure and happy), who may have serious financial problems, and who may be emotionally unprepared and incapable of adequately caring for a child/children alone.

The children of these broken families miss something vital in their emotional growth and strength when one parent is completely or usually absent from their daily lives. How many of these children will wind up with emotional problems because of feeling that one parent does not care about them? Think of the insecurity this type of feeling must cause. Is it any surprise that so many of these children turn to their peers or to false highs like drugs or alcohol or criminal activity to seek the emotional dependency and support they are not receiving in the home? In addition, children often find themselves unfairly caught in the middle of their parents' battles.

We Must Break the Pattern of Abuse in Relationships

We cannot, in good conscience, ever urge a person who has been battered, sexually abused, or otherwise abused by a mate to tolerate continued abuse, or to remain in such a relationship.

An abusive relationship is far worse than no relationship. Witnessing such abuse has a traumatic impact upon children as well.

Clearly, we must begin to focus on preventing persons from committing acts of domestic violence in the first place, and on finding successful ways to stop abusers from repeating such behavior.

Right now, the only realistic option we make available to families in which an abusive relationship exists is to end the relationship. This is probably an appropriate result. But in doing so, we add to the skyrocketing and frightening trend of breakup of families in our society.

When this author was executive director of a battered woman center, it was obvious that any number of the women and men involved in abusive relationships whom the center served wanted to remain together as marital (or live-in) partners. However, we usually had to encourage a separation because it was the only way we could find to ensure an end to the abuse.

I find myself having to ask the question which remains foremost in my mind as I think about domestic abuse situations.

WHAT IF THERE *IS* SOME WAY, SOME *SUCCESSFUL* WAY, TO BREAK THE PATTERN OF ABUSE IN RELATIONSHIPS?

Some batterers' programs appear to have a certain amount of success.

Maybe we need to enroll many more batterers in such programs.

Don't we need to focus our attention on searching for innovative solutions to domestic abuse problems—instead of concluding, in most cases, that the *only* appropriate resolution is to completely end the relationship?

I'm not saying that anyone should ever tolerate abuse. Of course, they shouldn't.

Often, when relationships end, no matter how bad such relationships were, we are left with two unhappy adults and unhappy children. A person whose abusive behavior has not been controlled or stopped is likely to find some other mate to abuse. A woman or man whose tendency to tolerate domestic abuse has not been effectively dealt with is likely to be attracted to and become involved with another abusive mate.

What, therefore, has been accomplished in the long run?

Our society is in great danger from trends like the breakup of families, domestic abuse, child sexual abuse and neglect, promiscuity, greed, immorality, materialism, loss of spirituality, violent crime, poverty, joblessness, drug and alcohol abuse, stress, and other social problems. Our solution to these problems has been aimed at helping victims after the abuse has occurred, at fixing wounds, jailing the criminals (or not taking the crimes seriously), providing financial and other help instead of long-term self-sufficiency and crime prevention. If we do not begin to focus our efforts beyond merely treating these harms once they have occurred—at *preventing* these abuses and crimes from occurring—we will simply watch the problems multiply.

As crime grows, as abuse increases, we, rightly, hire more people to process such cases, build more jails, and treat and bury more victims.

As family problems increase we add more courts, have more lawyers handle more divorces/custody battles, and hire more social workers, psychiatrists, and psychologists to deal with the emotional scars we have created.

About the only thing we do not do is fill more churches.

And what, I ask the reader, does this say about us, as a nation?

Religion, Morality, and Domestic Abuse

It seems to this author that if people were to live moral lifestyles, and to care about one another, this world would not be in the trouble it is.

Doing what is right (morally, religiously) is the only long-term solution to society's problems.

Therefore, a key aspect of any successful attack on domestic abuse must be the promotion of moral lifestyles.

Living any other type of lifestyle has been shown to cause a lot of misery in our society. The sorts of immoral behavior and attitudes which cause pain and suffering include: abuse; greed; sexual promiscuity; lying; materialism; theft; adultery; hatred and anger (when inappropriate); failure to love, care about other people; nonmarital sex; making idols out of people or things; violence; sins; lack of respect for other people, and; selfishness. All of these types of behavior are taught against in the teachings of the various religions in our society. Which, common sense, therefore, tells us, makes religion a powerful means, if used properly, of combating domestic and other abuse in our nation.

This author firmly believes that there are good and bad forces in society. If we deal with social problems from a purely humanitarian perspective and neglect to include in our decision making and theorizing the good concepts taught by religion, even well-meaning proposals may fail.

The overall solution to the domestic violence problem may lie in people becoming willing to conform their behavior and attitudes to the sorts of good principles and morality promoted by the various religions. There is no place for physical, sexual, or emotional abuse of persons in the system of justice promoted by moral and religious types of views. Obviously, there are religious concepts which promote patriarchal attitudes and those are erroneous. A realistic concept of religious principles would begin with the premise that it is intended for women and men to be equal and that no sort of abuse of persons can be tolerated in our society.

To deny that spirituality is an important part of humankind and must be an important part of the fight against domestic abuse would be foolish. Would it not be better for people with conflicting religious views to dialogue together more often to seek common ground and solutions to social ills? Churches can be a powerful force for good and for changing abusive behavior. Church leaders reach so very many people on a regular basis in our nation. They can emphasize the wrongness of abusive behavior and take a tough approach toward members of their congregations who are abusive. They can also provide emotional and other support for victims of abuse.

So many people give in to temptations (to be abusive, immoral, etc.) in our society. A greater emphasis on spiritual beliefs and behavior is needed.

Can we doubt, even for a moment, that if our people were to live by principles of religion and morality, our society would have far fewer problems and many more happy and contented people?

Chapter 16

NETWORKING

The key to a successful community effort to combat domestic violence is a well-organized, structured plan of networking among those public and private groups and individuals who are involved in handling domestic abuse problems. Anything less than a dedicated, organized, cooperative effort among the various groups and individuals who deal with such cases will not be very effective in fighting this large-scale social problem in each community. Situations in which various entities which come into contact with domestic abuse victims and abusers work at cross purposes or fail to actively network together to resolve individual abuse cases can result in failing to adequately help end the abuse.

This author recommends that communities do two major things to combat domestic violence. First, create a task force made up of various agencies and persons who handle domestic abuse cases to network together in the creation of a successful community-wide effort to fight such abuse. Second, conduct a thorough study of the extent and nature and potential solutions to the domestic abuse problem in the community at issues.

The Study

The study should address, in depth, issues including, but not limited to, these:

1. Can the criminal justice system be reformed to provide a more coordinated and effective response to individual situations of domestic abuse?

2. How bad is the domestic violence problem in the community? (This should consider not only reported cases, prosecuted cases, cases in which persons were arrested for abuse, and the like, but also an estimate of the extent of *unreported* domestic abuse incidents likely to have taken place in the study area. It is well known that most domestic abuse incidents never get reported to police, prosecutors, or any authority in a position to help the victim resolve the problem.)

3. What, specifically, is the role currently being played by the various persons and groups who deal with the domestic violence problem?

4. What changes should be made in the roles played by various persons and groups who deal with the abuse problem?

5. How effectively are the various agencies and persons who handle domestic violence problems in the community networking together to resolve the individual victim/abuser situations? (How well do the police, prosecutors, judges, battered women shelter staff, counselors, social workers, financial aid providers, educators, churches, etc. cooperate with each other and coordinate their responses to individual victimization situations?) Are there agencies or persons within the system who do not work well together in tackling abuse problems? Why is this happening? Are there conflicts of personality or of authority which are interfering with the effective fighting of abuse in the community? What can be done to change this?

6. What resources are lacking in the fight against domestic abuse? Police? Prosecutors? Counselors? Shelter space? Courts? Batterers' programs? Financial aid or other options for persons wanting to end their abuse? Training of professionals in handling domestic abuse cases? Community awareness?

7. Are there adequate treatment programs for batterers/abusers?

8. What data, if any, is available about the sex, age, financial status, education, children, marital status, etc. of the community's domestic abuse victims and abusers?

9. Is sufficient data being gathered regarding abuse history and personal information from victims of domestic abuse to adequately allow the system to address and make appropriate recommendations for solutions in individual cases of abuse?

10. What impact is domestic abuse having on persons who have been abused, have witnessed abuse, or have been abusers? (For example, lost work time/wages; medical/health costs; emotional/psychological problems; family breakdowns, including the impact on children; physical injuries, etc.)

11. What are the various specific responses of the agencies and individuals involved in combating domestic abuse in the community? (For example, how do police respond to domestic abuse service calls? What do prosecutors do when abuse arrests cross their desks? Are appropriate numbers of batterers being arrested? Are judges handing down appropriate sentences? Is too much dropping of charges, reducing of charges, and

failure to take such cases seriously taking place? Are victims of abuse getting more adequate counseling than that provided concerning their "options"—when needed? Are there any problems with any of the types of responses being provided within the criminal justice system to domestic abuse cases?)

12. Are the various individuals and agencies involved in the fight against domestic abuse properly and adequately perceiving the nature of the problem? (For example, do the police still, inappropriately, view such violence as a "family matter"?)

13. Are workable, adequate guidelines in place for the handling of domestic abuse cases in the police departments, prosecutors' offices, and elsewhere?

14. Are restraining orders available to victims of domestic abuse, and are these orders being issued by the courts? Are violations of them resulting in the arrest, prosecution, and sentencing of the abusers?

15. Is there a need to make any changes in the state's laws regarding domestic abuse cases? (For example, are police required to arrest abusers in certain cases? Are prosecutors required to prosecute? Is adequate funding for shelters and related needs available? Has a victim's consent been removed as an issue in domestic abuse battery cases? Are adequate prosecutors and courts and jails and related-needs provided for in the fight against domestic abuse? Does the legal system treat domestic abuse victims who kill their abuser in self-defense appropriately by having adequate laws regarding self-defense, permitting expert testimony about the Battered Woman syndrome, allowing into evidence the woman's history of abuse, and similar needs—to ensure that such women are not arrested, charged, or prosecuted or convicted for the commission of crimes like murder?)

16. What is the overall impact, on the community, of domestic abuse problems?

17. What additional changes need to be made in the handling of domestic abuse cases to better protect, and help the victims of abuse and to prevent their abusers from committing future acts of abuse?

Networking: If It's Broke, Let's Fix It

The failure of professionals who work with domestic abuse cases to network effectively to help victims and prevent/end abuse can have a dangerous consequence in such situations. Victims or perpetrators can end up dead or seriously injured or emotionally damaged for the rest of their lives.

The type of approach recommended below by this author is aimed at helping all parts of the system that work with domestic abuse cases network together for a more effective, better functioning program to help those families.

Creation of a Committee

A task force made up of representatives from the various agencies and individuals who fight domestic abuse in the community should be created for the purpose of effectively networking together to resolve domestic abuse problems.

The committee should meet regularly.

One of the purposes of the committee should be to conduct a study of the sort addressed above.

A second purpose should be to iron out problems which exist to inhibit cooperation. Interagency competition and fighting should be dealt with and eliminated. Nonrelevant differences of opinion should be buried. Attempts should be made to resolve important differences.

A third purpose should be to determine which agencies and/or persons will do which tasks in response to the domestic abuse problem.

A fourth purpose would be to set goals and to go about meeting them.

Lastly, the task force should create a public awareness campaign aimed at making victims of domestic abuse aware that they don't have to tolerate abuse, that there are people/agencies who will help them, that abuse is a crime, that programs exist to help abusers stop abusive behavior, and to create a positive public image about the programs which exist. The campaign should emphasize that the abuse is not likely to end unless the victims tell someone about the abuse and seek help.

Roles of the Various Agencies

1. Shelter Programs/Battered Women's Centers/Rape Crisis Centers

a. A safe place for victims to go to be away from their abusers.

b. Provide counseling, particularly that aimed at improving self-esteem and isolating options available to abused women.

c. Help with referrals for restraining orders, divorce and child custody suits, criminal proceedings against the abuser, education, employment, child care, transportation, counseling, financial assistance.

d. Provide support persons to accompany the victim to court proceedings, or just to be there to talk or provide emotional support when needed.

2. Police

a. Often the first to arrive at the scene of the domestic abuse crime; may need to get medical help/break up the parties/take action to protect the safety of the abuse victim and others.

b. Determine whether a crime has occurred (such as battery or assault or attempted murder); arrest the abuser; sign any criminal complaints issued by prosecutors.

c. Refer the victims to other services.

d. May have, in some cases, witnessed domestic violence.

e. Enforce restraining orders by arresting persons who violate such orders.

f. Collect evidence needed to make out effective court cases; collect statements from witnesses; sometimes take photographs of injuries suffered by abuse victims.

3. Prosecutors

a. Charge the batterer/abuser/rapist with any crimes which occurred, even if the abuse victim refuses to cooperate in the prosecution.

b. Provide support services for victims in the form of victim/witness services, financial compensation, etc.

c. Recommend serious sentences for domestic abuse crimes to judges.

d. Recommend deferred prosecution if an abuser enters and successfully completes an abuser program—when appropriate.

4. Judges

a. Treat domestic abuse/sexual abuse cases as serious crimes and issue appropriate sentences.

b. Avoid issuing fines which victim/children end up paying/suffering for.

c. Hear restraining order cases and sign restraining orders.

5. Social Services

 a. Provide financial assistance to victims/children.

 b. Provide counseling, as needed.

6. Abuser Programs

 a. Aim to end batterers' abusive behavior and attitudes.

 b. Show abusers what it is like not to be in control of their own lives.

7. Hospitals

 a. Provide medical assistance to victims.

 b. Recognize abuse as abuse instead of accepting stories from victims about falling down stairs, etc.

 c. Record abuse by taking pictures, x-rays, doctors' and nurses' notes.

 d. Be willing to be witnesses for victims in court.

8. Private Attorneys

 a. Handle divorce/custody cases, and civil lawsuits by abused women against abusers.

 b. Accept referrals from shelters and others.

9. Educators

 a. Educate society about the problems of domestic abuse.

 b. Educate domestic abuse victims to prepare them for jobs.

 c. Educate young people and members of the community about domestic abuse and sexual abuse in order to prevent it, locate cases involving it, and deal with it by making appropriate referrals.

10. Legislators

State legislatures, the U.S. Congress, county boards, city councils, and other elected officials must take strong actions to pass strong laws to prevent domestic abuse, punish domestic abusers, protect victims, and provide necessary services to such victims.

11. Churches

 a. Teach that abuse is wrong.

 b. Counsel families.

12. Counselors

a. Counsel victims of abuse.

b. Network with other providers of services needed by victims of abuse.

By making the above list, it is not the author's intent to limit the committee members or the participants in any domestic abuse programs to those specific resource groups/persons. Communities should add other agencies and persons, as they fit into their local situation, to this list, and determine the duties of those groups/people as well. For example, any task force should also include members of the public, and the press, and perhaps persons from various businesses.

Example of a Smoothly-Run Program Where there is Cooperation

What follows is an example of how a smoothly run system that networks effectively to help victims of domestic abuse might function:

1. The battered woman becomes aware of available help by hearing a speaker on television.

2. She is battered by her abuser.

3. The victim calls the police.

4. The police respond promptly and take the victim to the hospital to have her injuries treated, take photographs of her injuries, and make a police report about the incident. They also arrest the abuser and report this arrest to the prosecutor's office.

5. The hospital treats the victim and makes a medical record which includes information that her injuries were due to domestic abuse.

6. The police tell the victim about the battered women's center/shelter and take her or her children there (or get her consent to have the shelter call her and promptly have the shelter do so).

7. The center provides counseling to the victim, notifies her of her options, provides moral support, helps her apply for and obtain a domestic abuse restraining order promptly.

8. The judge signs the restraining order.

9. The abuser is now under a court order not to enter the home or to have any contact with the victim.

10. The victim sees an attorney whom the shelter staff referred her to about a divorce and gets a preliminary child custody order.

11. All parties involved (victim/abuser/police/prosecutor/judge) settle on deferred prosecution which involves abuser counseling.

12. The deferred prosecution does not work. The abuser again batters the victim.

13. The abuser is arrested for the new battery. He is found guilty, and sentenced by a tough judge to several months in jail with work-release privileges.

14. The abuser finally enters the batterers' program with a serious mind-set aimed at changing his abusive behavior.

15. The family either gets back together in a nonabusive relationship or the divorce is pursued and the system works to ensure the victim's safety and to keep her abuser away from her.

If the networking system breaks down, the following sorts of problems can result:

a. Police calm an abuser down and do not tell the victim of shelter services. The next time she is abused she does not call the police. The violence escalates. The victim kills the abuser in self-defense.

b. The police arrest a batterer. The prosecutor refuses to issue criminal charges. The police stop bothering to arrest abusers and the victims of abuse continue to be abused.

c. The judge issues a $200 fine against a batterer. The $200 is paid from the family food money. Because the abuser did not get jail time and/or abuser counseling, he knows he can freely continue to abuse the victim.

d. A shelter helps a battering victim obtain a restraining order but fails to refer her to an attorney for a divorce. No child custody order exists. The abuser takes the children, starts a divorce action, and gets custody.

e. Police take a battery victim whose arm has been broken to the hospital. Although she told the police her husband broke her arm, she tells the doctor that she fell down stairs and broke her arm. The hospital staff fails to talk to the police and does not question the victim's story. A false medical record is created.

CONCLUSION

It cannot be emphasized strongly enough that every community needs to have in place an effective network of agencies/individuals to prevent and handle domestic abuse cases. Effective means that the groups and persons involved work closely together to provide the best possible service to victims of abuse.

This author urges each community to create the sort of task force described above, to do the type of study recommended above, and to network effectively to prevent domestic abuse and to help its victims.

EPILOGUE

As I write this conclusion, I am struck by the similarity between the seemingly hopeless lifestyles faced by the battered women of today and yesterday and the youth gang members written about by David Wilkerson, John Sherrill, and Elizabeth Sherrill in *The Cross and the Switchblade* (Old Tappan, New Jersey: Fleming H. Revell Company, Spire Books, 1963). Members of both groups are faced with a choice—in order to survive. Gang members must choose to leave the gang lifestyle behind in order to protect their safety and integrity. Abused women must choose to end the abuse and violence in their lives—in order to be physically safe and emotionally stable.

The Reverend Wilkerson and the Sherrills described this well:

> I was driving back to Philipsburg, watching the odometer turn around and around keeping pace with the turnpike mile-markers as they crept past. Suddenly I was asking myself: "Suppose you were to be granted a wish for these kids. What would be the one best thing you could hope for?"
>
> And I knew my answer: that they could begin life all over again, with the fresh and innocent personalities of newborn children. And more: that this time as they were growing up they could be surrounded by love instead of hate and fear.
>
> But of course this was impossible. How could people already in their teens erase all that had gone before? And how could a new environment be made for them? "Is this a dream You have put into my heart, Lord? Or am I just weaving a fantasy for myself?"
>
> *They've got to start over again, and they've got to be surrounded by love.*
>
> The idea came to mind as a complete thought, as clearly as the first order to go to New York. And along with it came into my mind the picture of a house where these new kids could come. A really nice house, all their own, where they would be welcomed—welcomed and loved. They could live in their house any time they wanted to. The door would always be open; there would be lots and lots of beds, and clothes to wear, and a great big kitchen.
>
> "Oh, Lord," I said aloud, "what a wonderful dream this is! But it would take a miracle. A series of miracles such as I've never seen."

Wilkerson and the gang members he cared so deeply about did indeed receive the requested miracles. This minister eventually started Teen

Challenge centers across the nation modeled on the principles set forth in his book.

It is important to remember that it all began with one man's dream, one man's goal of helping boys and girls to find themselves by finding God. Perhaps this highlights the viewpoint that what matters most in life is not material things, but spiritual things.

Perhaps what this nation needs is a series of "miracles" to end the abuse of women, children, and men.

I think about Wilkerson's words and relate them to the plight of battered women and men in overcoming their abuse. Like the teenage gang members Wilkerson helped, battered women and men have "got to start over again, and they've got to be surrounded by love." Meeting that sort of goal as it relates to battered women and men in our society is most assuredly a major challenge. If we believe in this cause deeply enough and fight for it strongly enough, we will succeed.

Let me emphasize that there are *two* possible ways for an abused person to start over with a new lifestyle in which she or he is *SURROUNDED BY LOVE.*

The first is for her or him to end the abusive relationship and to develop friendships and positive relationships with people who are understanding, supportive, and loving.

The second is for the abuser to (through counseling, a batterers' program, or a heartfelt change of attitude and behavior) stop being abusive and become genuinely loving toward his or her mate. If this happens, the abused woman or man may decide to remain in the relationship and be surrounded by love.

It must be our sincere hope, as a caring society, that we will discover effective ways to *prevent* physical, verbal, and emotional domestic abuse so that fewer people will have their lives destroyed by such painful experiences. It is not enough for us to put Band-aids® on domestic abuse after it occurs—without undertaking the important goal of preventing it in the first place.

Lastly, I dedicate this book to the many women and men who have been battered, abused, or sexually assaulted by their mates, who, like me, either have found the courage or must find the courage to end the abusive relationship (or end the abuse in the relationship), and have found or will find the strength to go forward with their lives—SURROUNDED BY LOVE.

SARA LEE JOHANN